Verdi's

RIGOLETTO

OPERA CLASSICS LIBRARY™

Edited by Burton D. Fisher
Principal lecturer, *Opera Journeys Lecture Series*

Opera Journeys™ Publishing / Coral Gables, Florida

OPERA CLASSICS LIBRARY ™

• Aida • The Barber of Seville • La Bohème • Carmen
• Cavalleria Rusticana • Così fan tutte • Der Rosenkavalier
• Don Carlo • Don Giovanni • Don Pasquale • The Elixir of Love
• Elektra • Eugene Onegin • Exploring Wagner's Ring
• Falstaff • Faust • The Flying Dutchman • Hansel and Gretel
• L'Italiana in Algeri • Julius Caesar • Lohengrin
• Lucia di Lammermoor • Macbeth • Madama Butterfly
• The Magic Flute • Manon • Manon Lescaut
• The Marriage of Figaro • A Masked Ball • The Mikado
• Norma • Otello • I Pagliacci • Porgy and Bess • The Rhinegold
• Rigoletto • Der Rosenkavalier • Salome • Samson and Delilah
• Siegfried • The Tales of Hoffmann • Tannhäuser
• Tosca • La Traviata • Il Trovatore • Turandot
• Twilight of the Gods • The Valkyrie

WEB SITE: www.operajourneys.com   **E MAIL: operaj@bellsouth.net**

I have in mind another subject, which, if the police (censors) would allow it, is one of the greatest creations of modern theatre. The story is great, immense, and includes a character who is one of the greatest creations that the theatres of all nations and all times will boast.

The story is Le Roi s'amuse, and the character I mean is Triboulet.

  - Giuseppe Verdi, in a letter to librettest Francesco Maria Piave
    about Victor Hugo's "Le Roi s'amuse" as a subject for a new opera.

Contents

a *Prelude........*
to OPERA CLASSICS LIBRARY's *Rigoletto*

Verdi's *Rigoletto,* which premiered in 1851, began a new phase in the composer's artistic evolution and maturity: it signalled the introduction into his operas of bold and profound subjects, a greater dramatic and psychological depth, and an emphasis on spiritual values, intimate humanity and tender emotions; from *Rigoletto* onward, Verdi's operas possessed an expressiveness and an acute delineation of the human soul that had never before been realized on the opera stage.

OPERA CLASSICS LIBRARY explores Verdi's powerful music drama. The *Commentary and Analysis* offers pertinent biographical information about Verdi, the genesis of the opera and its original story source, its premiere and performance history, and insightful drama and character analysis.

The text also contains a *Brief Synopsis, Principal Characters in Rigoletto,* and a *Story Narrative with Music Highlight Examples,* the latter containing original music transcriptions that are interspersed appropriately within the story's dramatic exposition. In addition, the text includes a *Discography, Videography,* and a *Dictionary of Opera and Musical Terms.*

The *Libretto* has been newly translated by the Opera Journeys staff with specific emphasis on retaining a literal translation, but also with the objective to provide a faithful translation in modern and contemporary English; in this way, the substance of the drama becomes more intelligible. To enhance educational and study objectives, the *Libretto* also contains musical highlight examples interspersed within the drama's exposition.

The opera art form is the sum of many artistic expressions: theatrical drama, music, scenery, poetry, dance, acting and gesture. In opera, it is the composer who is the dramatist, using the emotive power of his music to express intense, human conflicts. Words evoke thought, but music provokes feelings; opera's sublime fusion of words, music and all the theatrical arts provides powerful theater, an impact on one's sensibilities that can reach into the very depths of the human soul.

Verdi's *Rigoletto* is certainly a glorious operatic invention, a powerful music drama that is a tribute to the art form as well as to its ingenious composer.

Burton D. Fisher
Editor
OPERA CLASSICS LIBRARY

RIGOLETTO

Opera in Italian in three acts

Music

by

Giuseppe Verdi

Libretto by Francesco Maria Piave
based on *Le Roi s'amuse* ("The King has a good time")
by Victor Hugo (1832)

Premiere at the Gran Teatro La Fenice, Venice,
March 1851

Commentary and Analysis

By 1851, the year of *Rigoletto's* premiere, the 38 year-old Giuseppe Verdi was acknowledged as the most popular opera composer in the world. He had established himself as the legitimate heir to the great Italian opera traditions that had dominated the first half of the nineteenth century, those *bel canto* operas of his immediate predecessors: Rossini, Bellini and Donizetti.

Viewing that opera landscape at mid-century, Verdi was unequivocally opera's superstar: Bellini died in 1835; Rossini had retired from opera compostion; and Donizetti died in 1848. In France at mid-century, Meyerbeer's grand opera spectacles were dominating the lyric theater (*Le Prophète* premiered in 1849), and in Germany, Wagner's *Lohengrin* premiered in 1850.

Verdi composed 15 operas during his first creative period, the years 1839 to 1851. His first opera, *Oberto* (1839), indicated promise and hope that an heir had surfaced to foster and continue Italian opera's great traditions, but his second opera, the comedy *Un Giorno di Regno* (1840), was received with indifference, a failure that has been attributed in part to his depression after the recent death of his wife and two children, and virtually signaled the end of his dreams to become an opera composer.

Nevertheless, Verdi's muse was awakened and re-inspired when he was presented with the libretto for *Nabucco*; the opera premiered in 1842 and was an immediate triumph, transforming Verdi overnight into an opera icon. He followed with *I Lombardi* (1843); *Ernani* (1844); *I Due Foscari* (1844); *Giovanna d'Arco* (1845); *Alzira* (1845); *Attila* (1846); *Macbeth* (1847); *I Masnadieri* (1847); *Il Corsaro* (1848); *La Battaglia di Legnano* (1849); *Luisa Miller* (1849); and *Stiffelio* (1850). Eventually, Verdi would compose 28 operas during his illustrious career, dying in 1901 at the age of 78.

The underlying theme at the foundation of Verdi's early operas concerned his patriotic mission for the liberation of his beloved Italy, at that time, suffering under the oppressive rule of both France and Austria. In temperament, Verdi was a true son of the Enlightenment, an idealist who possessed a noble conception of humanity. He abominated absolute power and deified civil liberty; his lifelong manifesto was a passionate crusade against every form of tyranny, whether social, political, or ecclesiastical.

Verdi was consumed by humanistic ideals and used his operatic pen to sound the alarm for Italy's freedom. Each of his early opera stories was disguised with allegory, metaphor, and irony, all advocating Italy's independence as well as individual freedom: the suffering and struggling heroes and heroines in his early operas were his beloved Italian compatriots.

For example, in *Giovanna d'Arco* ("Joan of Arc"), the French patriot Joan confronts the oppressive English and is eventually martyred, the heroine's plight synonymous with Italy's struggle against foreign oppression. In *Nabucco*, the suffering Hebrews enslaved by Nebuchadnezzar and the Babylonians were allegorically the Italian people, similarly in bondage by foreign oppressors.

Verdi's Italian audience easily read the underlying message he had subtly injected between the lines of his text and music. At *Nabucco's* premiere, at the end of the Hebrew slave chorus, "Va pensiero" ("Vanish hopes"), the audience actually stopped the performance with inspired nationalistic shouts of "Viva Italia." The *Nabucco* chorus became the unofficial Italian "National Anthem," the musical symbol of Italy's patriotic aspirations. Even the name V E R D I had become an acronym for Italian unification; V E R D I stood for *Vittorio Emmanuelo Re D'Italia*, a dream for the return of King Victor Emmanuel to rule a united Italy.

But as the 1850s unfolded, Verdi's genius had arrived at a turning point, a new period of artistic evolution and maturity. Verdi felt that his noble patriotic mission for Italian independence was soon to be realized, sensing the fulfillment of Italian liberation and unification in the forthcoming *Risorgimento,* the historic revolutionary event of 1861 that established the Italian nation as we know it today.

Verdi was satisfied that he had achieved his patriotic objectives, and decided to abandon the heroic pathos and nationalistic themes of his early operas. He was now seeking more profound operatic subjects: subjects with extreme boldness; subjects with greater dramatic and psychological depth; and subjects that emphasized spiritual values, intimate humanity and tender emotions. Verdi would be ceaseless in his goal to create an expressiveness and acute delineation of the human soul that had never before been realized on the opera stage, an endeavor that preoccupied him throughout his entire compositional career.

The year 1851 inaugurated Verdi's "middle period." It became a defining moment in his career, the moment when his operas would start to contain heightened dramatic qualities and intensities, an exceptional lyricism, and a profound characterization of humanity. Starting in this "middle period," Verdi's art flowered into a new maturity, and the result became some of the best loved operas of all time: *Rigoletto* (1851); *Il Trovatore* (1853); *La Traviata* (1853); *I Vespri Siciliani* (1855); *Simon Boccanegra* (1857); *Aroldo* (1857); *Un Ballo in Maschera* (1859); *La Forza del Destino* (1862); *Don Carlo* (1867); and *Aida* (1871). In his final works, he continued his advance toward a greater dramatic synthesis between text and music that would culminate in what some consider his greatest masterpieces: *Otello* (1887), and *Falstaff* (1893).

I n 1851, Verdi was approached by the management of La Fenice in Venice to write an opera to celebrate the Carnival and Lent seasons. In seeking a story source for the opera, Verdi turned to the popular romanticism of the French dramatist, Victor Hugo. Seven years earlier, in 1844, Verdi had a brilliant success with his operatic treatment of Hugo's *Hernani:* Verdi's *Ernani.*

Victor Hugo's play, *Le Roi s'amuse* ("The King has a good time"), premiered in 1832; it depicted the libertine escapades and adventures of the pleasure-loving King François I of France (1515-1547), but the drama featured as its primary force, an ugly, disillusioned and malicious hunchbacked court jester named Triboulet.

Hugo was a dynamic writer of the Romantic era, a period that coincides chronologically with the political and social turmoil that began with the storming of the Bastille and the outbreak of the French Revolution in 1789, to the last urban uprisings that erupted in almost every major European city in 1848.

Romanticism represented a pessimistic backlash against the optimism of the eighteenth century Enlightenment and the Age of Reason; Rousseau, a spokesman of Enlightenment ideals, had projected a new world order dominated by a heightened sense of individual freedom, civility and justice. But the Romanticists viewed those Enlightenment ideals of egalitarian progress as a mirage and illusion, a failure of elevated hopes and dreams that dissolved in the Reign of Terror (1792-94); that despair was reinforced by Napoleon's preposterous despotism and the ensuing wars, the post-Napoleonic return to autocratic tyranny and oppression, and the economic and social injustices nurtured by the Industrial Revolution.

The Reign of Terror totally destroyed any dreams of human progress remaining from the Enlightenment. Like the Holocaust in the twentieth century, those bloodbaths shook the very foundations of humanity by invoking man's deliberate betrayal of his highest nature and ideals; Schiller was prompted to reverse the idealism of his exultant "Ode to Joy" (1785) by concluding that the new century had "begun with murder's cry." To those pessimists — the Romanticists — the drama of human history was approaching doomsday, and civilization was on the verge of vanishing completely. Others concluded that the French Revolution and the Reign of Terror had ushered in a terrible new era of unselfish crimes in which men committed horrible atrocities out of love not of evil but of virtue. Like Goethe's *Faust,* who represented "two souls in one breast," man was considered a paradox, simultaneously the possessor of great virtue as well as wretched evil.

Romanticists sought alternatives to what had become their failed notions of human progress, and sought a panacea to their loss of confidence in the present as well as the future. Intellectual and moral values had declined, and modern civilization was perceived as transformed into a society of philistines, in which the ideals of refinement and polished manners had surrendered to a form of sinister decadence. Those in power were considered deficient in maintaining order, and instead of resisting the impending collapse of civilization and social degeneration, they were deemed to have embraced them feebly. As such, Romanticists developed a growing nostalgia for the past by seeking exalted histories that served to recall vanished glories: writers such as Sir Walter Scott, Alexandre Dumas, and Victor Hugo, penned tributes to past values of heroism and virtue that seemed to have vanished in their contemporary times.

Romanticists became preoccupied with the conflict between nature and human nature. Industrialization and modern commerce were considered the despoilers of the natural world: steam engines and smokestacks were viewed as dark manifestations of commerce and veritable images from hell. But natural man, uncorrupted by commercialism, was ennobled. So Romanticism sought escapes from society's horrible realities by appealing to strong emotions, the bizarre and the irrational, the instincts of self-gratification, and the search for pleasure and sensual delights.

Ultimately, Romanticism's ideology posed the antithesis of material values by striving to raise consciousness to more profound emotions and aesthetic sensibilities; for the Romanticists, the spiritual path to God and human salvation could only be achieved through idealized human love, individual freedom, and compassion for others.

Victor Hugo was an arch-Romanticist, the reigning king of the new literary forces, who was seeking to portray a truth of human existence. He was fascinated with extreme contrasts of human character, and boldly announced that he would no longer parade one-dimensional protagonists who were either all-virtuous, or all-villainous. Hugo now created new types of characters, complex and ambivalent personalities, whom he believed were truthful representation of flawed humanity; he would label these new repulsive characters "grotesque creatures."

In Hugo's play *Le Roi s'amuse,* in particular, he created his quintessential "grotesque creature," the ambivalent jester Triboulet, a tragic man with two souls: he was physically monstrous, morally evil, and a wicked personality, but also a man who was simultaneously magnanimous, kind, gentle and compassionate. Hugo's Triboulet — Rigoletto in Verdi's opera — was outwardly a deformed and physically ugly hunchback, a mean and sadistic man. But inwardly, Triboulet was an intensely human creature, a man filled with impassioned love that he showered boundlessly on his beloved daughter. (The name Triboulet is descriptive, derived from the French verb *tribouler,* meaning to guffaw, or to be noisy, hilarious, or boisterous.)

Verdi, an avid and intellectually curious reader, had read Hugo's *Le Roi s'amuse,* but certainly had never seen the play on stage. Hugo's play survived only the one night of its premiere in 1832; its next performance did not occur until 50 years later in 1882. Censors had banned the play from French, German, and Italian stages, compounding their criticism by determining its content overly abundant in immorality and repulsiveness.

A t the dawn of the 1850s, Verdi was now in his crusade to seek more intense operatic subjects, and he recognized in Hugo's play those sublime operatic possibilities to stir moral passions. He considered the Triboulet character a creation worthy of Shakespeare, a character who took human nature to its limits, and through whom, new levels of consciousness would be awakened. The character was a romanticist's dream hero: complex, twisted internally and externally, and saturated with picturesque misery.

Verdi wrote about the Hugo play — and the Triboulet character — to his favorite librettist of the time, Francesco Maria Piave, his librettist for his earlier operas *Ernani* and *Macbeth* — and later *La Forza del Destino:*

I have in mind another subject, which, if the police (censors) would allow it, is one of the greatest creations of modern theatre. The story is great, immense, and includes a character who is one of the greatest creations that the theatres of all nations and all times will boast.
The story is 'Le Roi s'amuse', and the character I mean is Triboulet.

There was intense hostility and animosity in the artistic marriage of Hugo's dramatic sources and Verdi's musical treatment of them. Earlier, Hugo had vigorously denounced Verdi's operatic adaptation of his play *Hernani* — as he would later do with *Rigoletto.* When Verdi's *Ernani* was staged in Paris, Hugo did everything within his power to prevent public production of what he considered a literary mutilation of his work, even unsuccessfully initiating legal action in the Paris courts to prohibit performances.

Hugo was admittedly resentful — and even envious and jealous — of Verdi's popularity, nevertheless, his complimentary comments about the famous Quartet from *Rigoletto*'s final act represented his reluctant admission of Verdi's operatic genius, as well as his tribute to the unique expressiveness of the operatic art-form. Hugo commented: "If I could only make four characters in my plays speak at the same time, and have the audience grasp the words and sentiments, I would obtain the very same effect." But it became Giuseppe Verdi, who would apply the evocative power of his music to Hugo's text that would ultimately provide immortality for Hugo's *Le Roi s'amuse.*

T he post-Napoleonic period was a period of political unrest and social tension. After the peace treaties evolving from the Congress of Vienna (1813-1815), the victorious allies established strong political alliances that would protect the status quo of their respective autocracies, all of which were being threatened by ethnic nationalism, and the Enlightenment appeal of individual liberty and freedom: new ideological forces evolving from the transformations caused by the French and Industrial Revolutions.

Truth is a coefficient of power, and the stability and continuity of the continental powers was directly proportional to their ability to control artistic truth. Censorship was their means to control ideas expressed in the arts, a government power that regulated and determined that nothing should be shown upon the stage that might undermine their authority, or in the least fan the flames of rebellion and discontent; it was an era in which revolutions and uprisings were erupting in every major European city. Indoctrination and propaganda controlled ideas; kings, ministers and governments all reflected an apparent paranoia, an irrational fear, and an almost pathological suspicion of any ideas they suspected of undermining their power. It was through censorship that nineteenth century monarchies exerted their power and determination to protect what they considered "universal truths": human progress would be reigned in through conservatism and the governmental control of ideas.

In France, Hugo's play *Le Roi s'amuse* became an immediate victim of censorship in action, a work that the authorities deemed subversive and therefore necessary to suppress. Despite the French Constitution's guarantee of freedom of expression, the censors' expressed their justification to ban the play, a judgment made without recourse or argument. The censorship authorities considered Hugo's subject immoral, obscenely trivial, scandalous, and its underlying theme subversive and threatening. Similarly, in Verdi's Italy, ruled in the 1850s by both France and Austria, censors controlled ideas expressed in the arts, and rejected and prevented performances of works whose ideas they considered in opposition to their power, or a threat to the social and political stability of their society.

The Verdi/Piave adaptation of Hugo's *Le Roi s'amuse* was initially titled *La Maledizione* ("The Curse"). Curses can have a powerful dramatic effect: in Wagner's *The Ring of the Nibelung,* Alberich's curse on the Ring after the Gods seize it from him provides the dramatic

— if not dynamic — thread for the entire four music dramas.

Likewise, in Verdi's opera, Monterone's curse on Rigoletto becomes the engine that drives the drama, its resolution the core and central dramatic force upon which the entire plot evolves. The aged Monterone appears before the Duke to vilify the licentious aristocrat for dishonoring his daughter, a rape by the debaucher for which Monterone invokes divine vengeance. After the Duke orders Monterone's arrest, Rigoletto impudently mocks the old man's anguish and agony, causing the outraged Monterone to curse both the Duke and Rigoletto: "Ah, siate entrambi voi maledetti!" ("You are both cursed!") But Monterone vents his full rage at the impudent Rigoletto: "E tu, serpente, tu che d'un padre ridi al dolore, sii maledetto!" ("And you serpent, who mock a father's agony, be accursed!")

Monterone's curse demonizes and condemns the slanderous Rigoletto, causing the jester to be overcome with incomprehensible fear; Monterone's curse becomes the engine that haunts Rigoletto throughout the drama, its music echoing ominously each time Rigoletto attempts to explain the tragic events that befall him: "Quel vecchio maledivami" ("That old man cursed me!") The dramatic effect of the curse is even more profound when each recurrence of the theme is in the same key and with the same instrumentation. The curtain falls three times to the underlying curse theme: at the end of Act I - Scene 1 when Monterone invokes the curse; at the end of Act I - Scene 2 after Rigoletto realizes that Gilda has been abducted; and at the very end of the opera when Gilda's death confirms that the curse has been fulfilled.

Verdi and librettist Piave were not naive about the censors' powers over their art; both were very much aware that their La Maledizione would provoke the Venetian censors. (Venice was then ruled by the Austrian Empire.) Indeed, just three months before the scheduled premiere of La Maledizione, composer and librettest became engaged in a battle to rescue their opera. The Austrian censors exploded in protest and totally rejected the work; they forbid its performance and expressed their profound regret that Verdi and Piave did not choose a more worthy vehicle to display their talents, specifically citing what they considered the story's revolting immorality and obscene triviality.

The church always considered curses antithetical, an invocation of a divine power to exact retribution through harm or misfortune. And the Austrian monarchy, a not-so-subtle theocracy uniting church and state, considered the curse theme to be blasphemously offensive and an impropriety. Nevertheless, Verdi and Piave remained hopeful that they might be able to bring the Hugo story to the opera stage without the censor's severe mutilation or alteration of the story's dramatic substance.

Their first concession to the censors was to change the opera's title from La Maledizione to Rigoletto; with the curse eliminated from its title, the opera now bore the name of its title character, a name derived from the French word "rigoler" ("to guffaw.") Another problem concerned the underlying story's portryal of the obscene and despicable misdeeds and frailities of the sixteenth century French King François I, a monarch who was dutifully depicted in the Hugo story as unconscionable, debauched and promiscuous. The censors cautioned that royal profligacy could not be exposed so conspicuously; that a king could not be portrayed as the seducer of a courtier's wife (Countess Ceprano); that a royal could not frequent a tavern and be seduced by a gypsy (Maddalena); and most of all, that a king could not be manipulated by a crippled jester and eventually become his intended assassination victim. Verdi's concession became the substitution of the Duke of Mantua for King François I: in effect, the Duke bore the anonymity of any Mantovani, an insignificant ruler of a petty state rather than an historic King of France; the story was now removed from the realm of French history to that of pure Italian fiction.

In addition, the relentless censors demanded that Rigoletto's daughter, Gilda, should be substituted with his sister; that the sleaziness of Sparafucile's Inn in the final scene should be altered to eliminate its aura of social evil; and finally, that they eliminate the repulsiveness of packing Gilda — or his sister — in a sack in the opera's final moments.

Defeat seemed to loom for the future of Verdi's newest opera. But a stroke of operatic Providence redeemed Verdi and saved *Rigoletto*. The Austrian censor, a man named Martello, was not only an avid opera lover, but a man who venerated the great Verdi as well. Martello made the final decision and determined that the change of venue from Paris to Mantua, and the renaming of the opera to *Rigoletto* adequately satisfied censor requirements.

From the point of view of both Verdi and Piave, *Rigoletto* had arrived back from the censors "safe and sound, without fractures or amputations."

The core of the *Rigoletto* drama concerns conflicts and tensions between parent and sibling: Rigoletto the father, and Gilda the daughter. Rigoletto imposes his incontrovertible will over Gilda's life, shielding her from the horrible evil and hostile world of which he is so familiar, a world of inhuman evil that he experiences daily at the court of the Duke of Mantua.

But Rigoletto is a powerful father figure, and consciously or subconsciously, father figures dominate almost all of Verdi's operas. In many scenarios, fathers and their offspring are seemingly alone in the world, or the fathers obsessively overprotect their children, or the fathers dominate their children tyrannically. In *Rigoletto,* Gilda and Rigoletto are threatened by another man, at times suggesting that their relationship is incestuous.

Were Verdi's powerful father figures metaphors for his subsconsious search for psychological truth? Verdi's relationship with his own father was full of constant conflict, tension and bitterness. He claimed that his father never understood him, at times even accusing his father of jealousy of his phenomenal artistic successes, and envy of his social and intellectual development. Those tensions virtually estranged Verdi from any affectionate relationship with his father, and his inner self yearned for fatherly affection and understanding. And Verdi's children died when they were very young, preventing him from lavishing parental affection on his own children, an ideal that lies deep within the soul of Italian patriarchal traditions.

Verdi used his art to express the paternal affection he yearned for, and the paternal affection he could never give to his own children; his unique musical language expressed the aftershock of those paternal relationships he lacked and yearned for in his own life.

In Verdi operas, there is a whole gallery of passionate, eloquent, and often self-contradictory father figures, fathers who are passionately devoted to, but are often in conflict with their children. Those father figures — almost always the darker voices of baritones or basses — express some of the most poignant moments in all of Verdi's operas: fathers who gloriously pour out their feelings with floods of intense emotion and passion.

And in many of those operas, fathers provide the emotional engine to drive the dramas and churn their cores. In *La Forza del Destino* ("The Force of Destiny"), the tragedy of the opera concerns a dying father who invokes a curse on his daughter, Leonora, as the heroine struggles in her conflict between her love for her father versus her love for Don Alvaro, the man who just killed her father. In *La Traviata*, Alfredo Germont's father develops a more profound respect and love for Violetta, the woman whose heart he has broken because of his errant son, than for the son for whose sake he has intervened; the elder Germont's "Piangi, piangi" ("I am crying"), represents Germont weeping for Violetta as if she were his own daughter. In *Don Carlo,* a terrifying old priest, the Grand Inquisitor, approves of King Philip II's intent to consign his son to death, the father agonizing and weeping in remorse and desperation over his son's perfidy. And in *Aida,* a father, Amonasro, uses paternal tenderness — as well as threats — to bend his daughter Aida to his will; she must betray her lover Radames because of her duty to country.

In Verdi operas, fathers are powerful and ambivalent personalities, men with tempestuous passions; suffering sons and daughters often sing "Padre, mio padre" in tenderness, or in terror, or in tears. And those same powerful fathers and their conflicts with their children intrigued Verdi to such an extent that throughout his life he would contemplate — but not bring to fruition — an opera based on Shakespeare's *King Lear,* one of the greatest of father figures: it is only coincidence that *Rigoletto* and *King Lear* are dramas about paternity that feature a court buffoon.

Rigoletto represents one of Verdi's quintessential father figures, and the jester's passionate paternal love for his daughter Gilda unquestionably inspired the magnificence of Verdi's music score for *Rigoletto*, music whose poignancy and emotional power dig deep into the human soul.

The essence of Rigoletto's character is his profound ambivalence; the two puppets he wears on his costume provide the metaphor for his dual personality. He is the victim of irreconcilable inner contradictions, tensions and conflicts. Like Goethe's *Faust,* Rigoletto possesses two souls in one breast: virtue and evil, but virtue is venerable and evil is repulsive.

As such, Rigoletto epitomizes the essence of Hugo's "grotesque creatures," those paradoxes of character in which one human being can be both beautiful and ugly, good or evil, or hero and villain. Like Dr. Jekyll and Mr. Hyde, or Shakespeare's Macbeth, Rigoletto epitomizes moral ambivalence and duality. But behind Rigoletto's obsessive hate and wickedness and evil, he is a man consumed by profound love.

Rigoletto's personal agony derives from his physical malformity: his hunchback and physical ugliness has set him aside as a curiosity, an object of humiliation in the discompassionate court of the Duke of Mantua; he is, like Merrick's *The Elephant Man,* a man condemned by nature to physical abornmality, and that ugliness causes society to look upon him as the "other," a fate in which a deformed man is condemned to a living hell.

In Act I - Scene 2, immediately following Rigoletto's encounter with Sparafucile, the assassin-for-hire, Verdi brilliantly provides Rigoletto with a platform to expose his anguished soul: the soliloquy "Pari siamo" ("We are the same!"), is essentially a narrative or recitative, but a segment that Verdi ingeniously injected with the poignant power of an aria. Rigoletto compares his own lethal evil to that of the sword-bearing assassin Sparafucile: "Pari siamo! Io la lingua, egli ha il pugnale" ("We are the same! I use my tongue, he uses the sword.")

Rigoletto proceeds to lament his destiny, a court jester who is commanded to provide laughter for others, which only intensifies his own personal sorrow. But in this self-introspective moment, Rigoletto admits that he has transformed into incarnate evil, a mean spirit who is unscrupulous, odious, brutish, and malicious: "Quanta in mordervi ho gioia!" (My only joy is to taunt you!")

Therefore, Rigoletto blames the courtiers for his malevolence: "Se iniquo son, per cagion vostra è solo." ("If I am vile, it is because of you.") Rigoletto blames his vile nature and his hatred of the world on the corrupt Duke and the court to whose service his deformity has condemned him. In his world, evil is the rule rather than the exception, so Rigoletto compounds the evil of the court, readily corrupting his master, and willingly aiding and abetting his master's seductions. In Act I -Scene 1, it is Rigoletto who suggests the means for the Duke to be free to remove any obstacle to his lust for the Countess Ceprano: imprison her husband, exile him, or even behead him. It is specifically Rigoletto's malice that inflames and provokes Count Ceprano and the courtiers to seek revenge against the villainous and spiteful court jester, and Rigoletto has been merciless in rubbing sadistic salt in Count Ceprano's wounds.

Rigoletto fights fire with fire. He feels justified in mocking the courtiers because they represent the other evils in the world, or perhaps because these men are not deformed with humps on their backs. As a jester and a merciless cynic, he is unconscionably ruthless and mean; each of the courtiers has at one time or another been his victim and has felt the jester's sting. And not even Rigoletto's false faith in his master can protect him from those he has scorned; in the end, Rigoletto becomes the victim of his own scorn.

Although Rigoletto hates his corrupt and evil surrounding world, he is dominated by his own self-hatred and fully realizes that he is as evil as those he hates. Because of his deformity, Rigoletto has become a mean, bitter and spiteful man, seeking revenge against humanity and Nature.

Rigoletto's caustic treatment of Monterone, the father whose daughter was raped, is nothing less than wicked and cruel; he sneers with gleeful contempt at this unhappy father, deriding a man who is outraged by his daughter's victimization by the Duke. But Rigoletto's heartlessness toward Monterone is the crux of the story, the story's magnificent dramatic irony; it is specifically Rigoletto's callousness toward another man's love for his own daughter and her honor, that becomes the essence of Rigoletto's own tragedy with his own daughter.

Nevertheless, Rigoletto has his one moment of glory, the triumph of his vengeance against the world. In Act III, after Sparafucile delivers the sack to Rigoletto, he erupts into vengeful joy: "Ora mi guarda. o mondo! Quest'è un buffone, ed un potente è questo!. Ei sta sotto i miei piedi! È desso! Oh gioia!" ("Now world look at me! This is a jester, and indeed a man of power! And he remains under my foot! It is true! What joy!") But of course Rigoletto's moment of joy is immediately shattered when he hears the voice of the Duke in the distance: "La donna è mobile qual piuma al vento," an ominous signal that his revenge has been betrayed.

The counter-force to Rigoletto's hatred of the Duke and the courtiers is his passionate love for his daughter, Gilda: that love represents the essential ambivalence in his character. The misshapen jester keeps just one part of his evil nature pure, a sensitive and passionate love that he reserves for his beloved daughter. The power of that love serves to redeem and reconcile him, at times forcing us to vacillate in our feelings about him; on the one hand, he repels us as a man of evil, but on the other hand, we are gradually drawn to him in sympathy, empathizing with his very human suffering.

Rigoletto keeps Gilda isolated from the vice of Mantua. He teaches her only virtue and goodness, and nurtures her in innocence, faith and chastity. His greatest fear is that she may fall into evil, because being evil himself, he knows what it is, and he knows what suffering it causes. Therefore, Rigoletto's treasured Gilda is secluded behind high walls, hidden, shielded and sheltered from the realities of the wicked world surrounding her. She has been commanded never to leave the house except to go to church under the protection of Giovanna, her nurse. Gilda, the light of Rigoletto's life, has become his bird in a cage, a victim of a father's overprotection that can almost be interpreted as an incestuous perversion of a father-daughter relationship disguised as pure paternal love.

On the surface, Gilda is naïve, simpleminded, and an angelic innocent, but her romantic fantasies and her unconscious erotic desires and yearnings all come to life in the ecstasy of her first love. Gilda becomes overwhelmed — and passion overcomes reason — when she meets her first suitor, the Duke in the disguise of a poor student, a man she accepts at face value and without question.

In a certain sense, as the plot progresses, sweet Gilda is not all that sugary, nor is she exactly snow-white in her purity, certainly not a sainted, innocent maiden. Gilda can be seen as nothing more or less than a mutinous — if not rebellious child — who defies parental authority. Gilda not only falls in love with an anonymous man she does not know, but surrenders to him consensually, what Rigoletto will interpret as the Duke's rape of his daughter.

From the very beginning of this story, Gilda is a disobedient daughter: she lies to her father in Act I when she fails to respond to his interrogation and reveal to her father that she has been followed home from church by a stranger; she will further disobey her father in the final act by returning to the scene of her lover's treachery and watch with broken-hearted incredulity as the libertine Duke tries to seduce Maddalena, Sparafucile's gypsy sister and accomplice. But Gilda has surrendered her heart to her new-found lover: in her "Caro nome" aria, she vows eternal constancy and her determination to be true to her lover until her last breath. Gilda will not only surrender her heart to a man unworthy of such devotion, but she will surrender her life for him willingly, and with courage and resolution. Afterwards, she will ask her father's forgiveness not only for what she has done, but for the man who betrayed her.

The supreme irony of this father-daughter relationship is that Gilda has even been shielded from Rigoletto himself: she has no knowledge of who her father really is, or what he does. Therefore, perhaps the most pathetic moment of the opera occurs in Act II when the freshly ravished Gilda sees her father in his court jester costume for the first time; it is indeed a tragic moment in which shame overcomes both father and daughter.

I t is Monterone's curse that is invoked not only on Rigoletto in his role as the mocking, cynical court jester, but is also intended to strike Rigoletto as a father. Rigoletto, just like Monterone, becomes the tragic father who likewise loses his treasured daughter to the evil of the court and the outside world. In the irony of this story, the same Duke whom Rigoletto urged on to indiscriminate libertine escapades, dishonors Rigoletto's daughter, striking down the jester in his role as father in exactly the same manner as Monterone.

Rigoletto challenges defeat with denial. He is unable to face the bitter truth that the Duke ravished Gilda, and certainly is unable to believe that she became enamoured by the Duke and willingly consented to consummate their love. Rigoletto is unable to believe that the evil in the world has invaded his life, or that the pedestal upon which he has placed his daughter has crumbled.

Rigoletto can only vindicate himself by exacting justice through personal revenge on the Duke. Revenge is the failure of reason: it is when savagery overcomes the savage; when hatred is recycled; and when inherent morality transforms into chaos. Rigoletto justifies his revenge when he responds to Sparafucile's request to know the victim's name: "Egli é Delitto, Punizion son io" ("He is Crime, I am Punishment"), revenge justified as an eye for an eye rather than turning the other cheek. In the end, the poignant tragedy of this story is pure irony, because revenge has been foiled when this vanquished father finds himself alone with the corpse of his beloved daughter, and the jester is reminded again of Monterone's haunting and portentous curse.

In that final scene, Verdi's music soars upwards, rising to heaven with Gilda. Screams and melodramatic passion are superfluous as Rigoletto's beloved Gilda dies in her father's arms, a cathartic and poignant moment, but yet another impassioned portrayal of father-daughter suffering and agony. Hugo ended his drama as Triboulet screams his final pathetic anguish: "I've killed my daughter." In Verdi, Rigoletto's final anguish is: "Ah! La maledizione" ("Ah! The curse"). For Rigoletto, Monterone's curse, not his own evil actions, is the cause of his personal tragedy; Rigoletto's disaster and catastrophe are revealed in the fury and frustration of his final outburst, an expression of his ultimate impotence and the failure of his will.

The Duke is that quintessential operatic cad so familiar to opera-lovers in the roles of Don Giovanni, Pinkerton, or Baron Ochs. He is unquestionably a villainous libertine, a man with a devil-may-care philosophy, and a skirt-chaser who lives for conquest. His signature mottoes are expressed in his two arias: "Questa o quella per me pari sono" ("This woman or that woman, they're all the same"), and "La donna è mobile" ("All women are capricious.")

The Duke, like Rigoletto, is also an ambivalent character. In Act II, the Duke expresses apparent heartfelt tenderness as he laments his presumed loss of Gilda, a longing certainly inconsistent with the crudeness of his historical behavior. In that short, transitory moment of ambivalent sentiment and compassion, the repugnant rake surrenders to his profound inner feelings, however fleeting or momentary those emotions may be; at this moment, he praises Gilda as the one person in the world who had inspired him with a lasting love and the fulfillment of his desire: "Parmi veder le lagrime scorrenti da quel ciglio" (I seem to see tears running from those eyes.")

Sparafucile, although a minor character in the drama, also possesses ambivalent attributes. He is a prideful and workmanlike professional assassin who promises satisfaction to his clients. He approaches his profession with a sense of honor, becoming highly indignant when his sister Maddalena pleads for the Duke's life; after all, he has accepted a fifty percent downpayment to complete the job, and he cannot reneg on his promise. He asks Maddalena: does she think he is a crook? And when Maddalena suggests that he dispatch Rigoletto instead of the Duke, he rants that she has perhaps lost her senses, because she knows that he would never double-crosses a client. Yet Sparafucile has a sentimental streak in him. Maddalena's tears weaken him, and they become the force that persuades him to agree to kill a substitute, should one appear before midnight.

After Verdi launched his "middle period" in 1851 with *Rigoletto,* his quest for more intense human passion on the lyric stage continued into his next opera, *Il Trovatore.* In this opera, his central character became the swarthy and ominous gypsy mother, Azucena, a character obsessed with revenge, who dominates the opera story as she savagely recounts the vivid horror of how her mother was brutally led to execution.

For Verdi's nineteenth century audiences, archetypal, or beautiful heroines and handsome heroes were the only acceptable characters to be seen onstage: villains could be ugly, but they could only be secondary figures. Nevertheless, with Rigoletto and Azucena, Verdi introduced exciting wicked people with tragic souls: shocking and repulsive figures. Verdi proved that in making these underdogs of society major protagonists, he was willing to go quite far in his search for the bizarre. In certain respects, these characters, consumed by bloodthirsty passions, represented the prelude to realism in opera: the *verismo* that would highlight the Italian opera genre toward the end of the nineteenth and beginning of the twentieth centuries.

Verdi understood well that common man suffers the need for revenge as genuinely as kings, gods and heroes. As his "middle period" of composition began, he was determined to introduce suffering humanity to the opera stage: Rigoletto, the cynical and mocked hunchback, and Azucena, a hideously ugly and reviled gypsy. For both characters, the mainspring of their actions is revenge. But for both, revenge leads to a tragic irony: Rigoletto's actions bring about the death of his own daughter, killed by the assassin he hired to murder the Duke; Azucena causes the death of her adored surrogate son Manrico, first by admitting under torture that she is his mother, and second, by hiding from her arch-enemy di Luna, the fact that he and Manrico are actually brothers, an admission that could have saved Manrico.

Rigoletto and Azucena are thus the male and female faces of revenge that become defeated: a revenge that ultimately brings about fatal injustice and tragedy. Both operas, *Rigoletto* and *Il Trovatore,* are therefore masterpieces of dramatic irony. The final horror for both Rigoletto and Azucena is that these protagonists believe they are striking a blow for justice. Essentially, Rigoletto's final justification is "Egli è Delitto, Punizion son io" ("He is Crime, I am Punishment"); Azucena repeats her mother's plea "Mi vendica." ("Avenge me.") However, in the end, both fail and witness their children lying dead, and the only difference between them is that Rigoletto may live on in agony, while Azucena will surely die at the stake as did her mother.

V erdi composed *Rigoletto* at almost the identical time that Wagner was theorizing his *Gesamtkunstwerk,*the ideal that the opera art form was the sum of its parts; a total artwork that integrated its text, music, and all the other theatrical elements. For the next quarter-century, Wagner's lyric compositions would revolutionize and transform opera into music drama: *The Ring of the Nibelung, Tristan und Isolde, Die Meistersinger*, and *Parsiful.*

Likewise, Verdi was intuitively evolving his art form from its *bel canto* origins toward a more integrated form of music drama: *Rigoletto* represented the beginning of that evolution. Nevertheless, *Rigoletto* contains many links to the Italian *bel canto* traditions; there are many "hit-parade-style" set-pieces, and many dance-style rhythmic accompaniments, internal structures that were certainly anathema to the Wagnerian ideal. But *Rigoletto* is a transition opera, in which Verdi bound its musical and textual elements into a more profound organic unity than he had ever achieved in any of his earlier operas. There is a more perfect balance between lyrical and dramatic elements, and the orchestra is not just the traditional accompanist, but an integral part of the drama. In addition, *Rigoletto* contains many beautiful melodic inventions that link recitative to aria, eliminating that no-man's land or barrier between the end of an aria, and the beginning of another set-piece; all of *Rigoletto*'s music is essentially unified, and as a result, each scene swiftly speeds the opera from one breathtaking climax to another.

In essence, the success of *Rigoletto*'s musical inventions became Verdi's springboard for his Italian music drama of the future, particularly his final four masterpieces: *Don Carlo, Aida, Otello,* and *Falstaff.* But *Rigoletto*'s greatness lies in the vitality of its music, a veritable treasure chest of glorious and lush music possessing powerful passion. Verdi's new musical language for *Rigoletto* was now speaking with a new momentum, an intensity and energy that at times seems to overflow with violence, raging emotions, and even murderous glee.

Rigoletto is an Italian opera to the core, and in that sense, it reverently and piously follows the great traditions of the genre: it is a work in which the voice reigns supreme, and it is saturated with beautiful melody and music with vivid beauty and spontaneous power; the Duke's "Questa o quella" and "La donna è mobile," Gilda's "Caro nome" and confessional "Tutte le feste," Rigoletto's "Pari siamo" and "Cortigiani," the "Si vendetta" duet, and, of course, the final act "Quartet," the latter universally acknowledged a marvel of musical invention, in which the diverse conflicts of the characters are exposed in a brilliant, coherent musical unity.

And although *Rigoletto* provides the vocally charismatic roles of the Duke (tenor) and Gilda (lyric coloratura), it is the title role of Rigoletto (baritone) that remains one of the greatest operatic roles ever composed. Verdi developed the high baritone voice for his earlier *Macbeth* (1847), pushing the expressiveness of the lower voice range even higher through his musical scoring. But for *Rigoletto*, Verdi transcended any of his previous musical inventions for the high baritone voice; the role is saturated with a full range of vocal expression, from moments of ecstatic rapture, to moments of profound agony.

V erdi himself described *Rigoletto* as revolutionary, if not a landmark in his career: "the best subject as regards theatrical effect that I've ever set to music. It has powerful situations, variety, excitement, pathos; all the vicissitudes arise from the frivolous, rakish personality of the Duke. Hence, Rigoletto's fear, Gilda's passions...."

Rigoletto always remained Verdi's favorite work, a work saturated and integrated with strong dramatic and lyric beauty, poignant expressions of emotion and pathos, despair, romantic agonies, passions of love, and, of course, that tempestuous fury that churns the opera: revenge.

Rigoletto is one of Verdi's supreme lyrical masterpieces. Beginning with *Rigoletto,* the composer would surge forward into his "middle period" to create some of the most enduring works of the operatic canon, operas he composed in a totally new spirit with bolder subjects and characterizations that would possess greater dramatic and psychological depth.

Nevertheless, Verdi's *Rigoletto* represents, in effect, the sum and substance of Italian opera, and, as such, it survives as one of opera's supreme masterpieces; it is a magical chemistry of great music and text and that expresses profound human emotion, passion and pathos.

RIGOLETTO

Principal Characters in Rigoletto

Brief Synopsis

Story Narrative with Music Highlight Examples

Principal Characters in Rigoletto

Rigoletto, a court jester	Baritone
Gilda, Rigoletto's daughter	Soprano
Duke of Mantua	Tenor
Giovanna, Gilda's nurse	Soprano
Sparafucile, a hired assassin	Bass
Maddalena, Sparafucile's sister	Soprano
Monterone, a nobleman	Bass

Count Ceprano, Countess Ceprano, Borsa,
Marullo, and courtiers

TIME: 16th century
PLACE: The city of Mantua, Italy

Brief Synopsis

Rigoletto is a grim and brutal melodrama. Rigoletto, deformed and hunchbacked, is a jester in the sixteenth century Court of the Duke of Mantua. Rigoletto mocks and outrageously insults the husbands and fathers of his master's amorous conquests, eventually provoking the noble Monterone, whose daughter had been raped by the Duke, to invoke a father's curse on him; the curse haunts Rigoletto throughout the drama, and ironically, the curse is fulfilled when tragedy overcomes Rigoletto.

Rigoletto has a young daughter, Gilda, whom he overprotects by secluding her from the outside world. Unknown to Rigoletto, Gilda falls in love with the Duke after she meets him in church; he is disguised as a poor student. The courtiers of the Mantuan court, seeking revenge against the despised court jester, believe Gilda to be Rigoletto's mistress. They conspire to abduct her and deliver their prize to the libertine Duke.

Rigoletto finds Gilda in the palace and vows revenge against the Duke after he learns that he has raped his beloved daughter; he hires the professional assassin, Sparafucile, to murder the Duke. Sparafucile's sister and accomplice, Maddalena, becomes infatuated with the Duke and persuades her brother to fulfill his murder contract by killing the next person who enters their inn.

Gilda sacrifices her life for her new-found love and becomes the victim of Sparafucile's sword. In a tragic irony of failed revenge, the corpse delivered to Rigoletto is his own beloved daughter, Gilda, not the Duke of Mantua.

Story Narrative and Music Highlight Examples

Prelude:

A short prelude, somber, ominous, and menacing, musically presages the forthcoming tragedy. In Act I - Scene 1, after Monterone condemns the Duke for raping his daughter, Rigoletto mocks the aged nobleman. In return for his insolence, Monterone invokes a father's curse on Rigoletto.

The main musical motive of the prelude is the curse theme that underscores Rigoletto's fear and horror, and haunts him throughout the drama: "Quel vecchio maledivami!" *("That old man cursed me!")*

Andante sostenuto

Act 1 - Scene 1: A salon in the Duke of Mantua's palace

An elegant assemblage of courtiers, ladies, and pages, are gathered in a magnificent salon in the Duke's palace. The festive air is accented by lighthearted, elegant dance music heard from another room of the palace. The trivial gaiety is a profound contrast to the grotesque reality of the scene, which is saturated by decadence, banality, evil and depravity.

Dance Music:

Allegro con brio

The libertine Duke of Mantua strolls through the crowd while in conversation with Borsa, one of his courtiers. He enthusiastically speaks about a beautiful young girl he saw in church, whom he has been pursuing incognito for the past three months. He relates how he followed her to her small home located in a narrow lane in a remote part of the city, but he has been confounded by the appearance of a mysterious man who visits her every evening.

The Duke's attention wanders to a group of women who pass before him. Among them is the Countess Ceprano, whose beauty he praises, and for whom he has implacable lust. He is heedless to Borsa, who cautions him that her husband, the Count Ceprano, must not overhear his amorous intentions toward his wife.

The Duke responds to Borsa's caution by expounding his libertine, chauvinist philosophy about women: "Questa o quella per me pari sono" (*"This woman or that woman, they're all the same."*) For the cynical Duke, one pretty woman is the same as any other; today this one pleases him, tomorrow another. He speaks of fidelity with scorn: "a tyranny of the heart." And he affirms his freedom to love according to his whims, while arrogantly ridiculing the anger of cuckolded and jealous husbands.

"Questa o quella per me pari sono"

Allegretto
DUKE

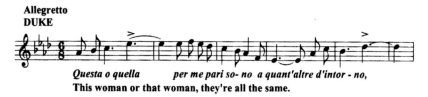

Questa o quella   per me pari so- no a quant'altre d'intor - no,
This woman or that woman, they're all the same.

Indifferent to Count Ceprano's jealousy, the Duke fervently continues his flirtations with the Countess, kissing her hand and telling her that he is intoxicated by his passion for her. The Duke and Countess Ceprano wander off casually to an adjoining room.

Rigoletto, the hunchbacked court jester, arrives. Immediately, he begins to taunt and provoke the furious and raging Count Ceprano, adding fuel to his outrage by implying that the Duke is enjoying the willing favors of his wife. Rigoletto then goes off to follow the Duke and the Countess Ceprano.

The courtier Marullo arrives. To the merriment of the other courtiers, Marullo announces the news that he has discovered that the ugly old jester has a mistress, a woman whom he visits every night. The courtiers react in disbelief, suggesting to Marullo that pandering by this sexually repulsive hunchback must surely be an hilarious joke.

The Duke returns to the festivities, followed by Rigoletto. He confides to Rigoletto that the Countess Ceprano would be a wonderful conquest, however, her husband is an impediment to his desires for her, and he would like to get rid of him. The malevolent Rigoletto adds fuel to the fire and casually suggests prison, exile, or even execution for the Count, saying with nonchalance: "so what, what does it matter?" Ceprano overhears their nefarious conversation and fumes with revenge, barely able to restrain himself from drawing his sword against the malevolent Rigoletto.

The Duke scolds Rigoletto, suggesting that his jesting has been excessive; nevertheless, the jester feels secure that the Duke will always protect him. All the courtiers have at one time or another been victims of the malevolent derision of the contemptuous court jester. But this time, Rigoletto's jibes at Count Ceprano have pushed the envelope, and at Ceprano's urging, the courtiers readily agree to meet later that evening to plot revenge against Rigoletto. Their revenge will be ironical; they will abduct Rigoletto's "mistress," following the same advice the vicious jester just offered his master.

The stern voice of the aged Count Monterone is heard from outside, demanding to be admitted. Monterone confronts the Duke and denounces the profligate libertine for seducing his daughter. Rigoletto mocks and ridicules the old man, but Monterone continues his protest and declares that dead or alive, he will haunt the Duke for the rest of his days.

In response, the Duke orders Monterone's arrest. But the relentless Rigoletto continues to insult the outraged father, ultimately inflaming Monterone to curse both the Duke and the villainous court jester. Monterone, the austere voice of divine justice, then invokes his total fury on Rigoletto: "E tu, serpente, tu che d'un padre ridi al dolore, sii maledetto!" ("And you, serpent, who mock a father's agony, be accursed.") It is Monterone's second curse, directed solely at Rigoletto, that terrifies the jester.

The courtiers resume their festivities as Monterone is led off by guards. Rigoletto trembles with fright and recoils in fear; Monterone's curse has become firmly implanted in his soul.

Act I - Scene 2: A dark and deserted street

Rigoletto walks toward his home, almost totally disguised by his cloak. He has become paranoid by Monterone's curse and expresses his haunting fear: "Qual vecchio maladivami!" ("That old man cursed me!")

Rigoletto is followed by an ominous figure, who introduces himself as Sparafucile, a professional assassin-for-hire. Sparafucile describes his profession with the self-conscious rectitude of an honest tradesman. He offers Rigoletto his services at reasonable fees should he ever need to get rid of any rival for the young woman he keeps under lock and key.

Sparafucile's theme:

Sparafucile explains the intrigues of his trade to Rigoletto; he and his sister, a gypsy temptress, lure their victims to their Inn and then dispose of them. Rigoletto dismisses Sparafucile, indicating no present need for his services, but he indeed makes a point of learning how the assassin can be found should a future need arise.

Alone, Rigoletto is again haunted by returning thoughts of Monterone's curse. He then reflects on his chance meeting with the assassin for hire, comparing himself as his equal: "Pari siamo! Io la lingua, egli ha il pugnale" ("We are the same! I use my tongue, he uses the dagger.") Both men indeed share evil: both men are paid to wound their victims with their lethal weapons; one with his tongue, the other with his dagger.

"Pari siamo"

Adagio
RIGOLETTO

Pa - ri   sia - mo!   io   la lin - gua,   egli ha il pugna - le.
We are the same! I use my tongue, he uses the dagger.

In his soliloquy, Rigoletto curses fate and nature for bringing him into the world as an ugly and deformed man. He further blames the vile courtiers as the cause of his own wickedness, hatred and evil. But again his mood is shaken as Monterone's curse returns to haunt his thoughts. Suddenly, the tender echo of flute music returns his thoughts to his beloved daughter, Gilda.

Rigoletto enters the courtyard of his house. Gilda rushes joyfully to embrace her father.

Gilda welcomes Rigoletto:

Allegro vivo

Gilda senses her father's sadness; he is uneasy and agitated. Rigoletto turns to panic, and immediately asks Gilda if she has been out of the house, fearing that she would fall victim to one of the courtiers or the evils of the city.

Gilda tries to assuage her father's anxiety by expressing her deep love for him. Then she asks to know more about him and her family. Why does her father never tell her his name? When she asks about her mother, Rigoletto is unable to speak of his grief at her loss.

"Deh non parlare al misero"

Andante
RIGOLETTO

Deh non parla-re al mi-se-ro   del suo   perdu-to be   - ne.
Don't speak of the grief of that terrible loss.

Rigoletto passionately explains to Gilda that she is his only treasure left in this world. Preoccupied by fears, Rigoletto turns to the nurse Giovanna and reminds her to carefully protect his beloved child; Gilda is to remain within the walls of their home and never to venture into the town except on that one day when the nurse is to accompany her to church.

"Ah! Veglia o donna"

Allegro moderato assai
RIGOLETTO

Ah! Veglia o don - na,questo fio-re che a tè pur - ro confi- dai.
Lady, guard this innocent flower who I place in your trust,

Noises are heard from the street. Rigoletto panics and rushes out to investigate. After he leaves, the Duke slips into the courtyard, sees the nurse Giovanna, and throws her a purse to buy her silence. When Rigoletto returns, the Duke hides.

Unable to allay his fears and suspicions, Rigoletto questions Gilda if anyone ever followed her from church. Gilda responds negatively, assuring her father that he need not fear for her safety; her mother — an angel in heaven — is always protecting her.

Rigoletto bids a touching farewell to Gilda, his parting words "mia figlia" ("my daughter"), overheard by the hiding Duke; the revelation that she is his daughter surprises the Duke.

After Rigoletto departs, Gilda confesses to Giovanna her remorse at not having confided to her father that she has frequently been followed from church by a handsome young man. As she reveals her love for this mysterious suitor — " t'amo" ("I love you") — the Duke emerges from hiding. He embraces Gilda, and then explodes into a rapturous declaration of his love for her.

"È il sol dell'anima"

Andantino
DUKE

È il sol dell 'anima, la vita è a-more sua vo - ce è il palpito del nos-tro core.
Love is love, the sun of the soul, its voice the throb of our hearts.

Gilda tries feebly to resist the Duke's ardor, but she surrenders. In response to Gilda's curiosity, the Duke tells her that his name is Gualtier Maldè, a poor and struggling student.

The voices of Borsa and Ceprano — preparing the courtier's intrigue to abduct Rigoletto's mistress — cause Giovanna to warn the lovers that someone is outside. Gilda is also fearful that her father may be returning and insists that her new-found lover depart. Gilda and Gualtier Maldè — the Duke — sing a passionate farewell.

"Addio, addio, speranza ed anima"

Alone, Gilda sighs joyfully about the poor student she has fallen in love with: Gualtier Maldè, a name that is now carved in her heart.

"Caro nome"

Meanwhile, the courtiers —— disguised and masked — have assembled in the dark night outside Rigoletto's house. From hiding, they notice Gilda on the balcony and comment on the beauty of "Rigoletto's mistress."

Rigoletto unexpectedly returns and runs into the courtiers. They calm his fears and suspicions by telling him that their mission is to abduct Ceprano's wife for the Duke. Rigoletto erupts into perverse delight at the intrigue; he points them to Ceprano's house and offers them his help.

The courtiers insist that Rigoletto must also be masked. Thoroughly confused and blinded by the mask, Rigoletto unwittingly holds a ladder for the courtiers against what he believes to be the wall of Ceprano's house, but in reality, he is holding the ladder against his own house.

The courtiers enter Rigoletto's house and abduct Gilda.

A moment later, Gilda's cries for help are heard in the distance, followed by shouts of victory from the escaping courtiers. But Rigoletto, his ears covered by the mask, hears nothing. Now thoroughly confused and bewildered, he tears off the mask and discovers that he is in his own courtyard. He notices Gilda's scarf on the ground, and then notices that the door of his house is wide open. Frantic with fear, he rushes into his house and finds that Gilda has disappeared.

He emerges from the house dragging the terrified Giovanna. He staggers in shock, realizing that he has helped bring disaster upon himself. In agony, he remembers Monterone's curse, and then blames the curse for his misfortune: " Ah! La maledizione!" ("Ah, the curse!") Then, Rigoletto faints.

Act II: A drawing room in the Duke's palace

The Duke is agitated and distraught. He had returned to Rigoletto's house, but instead of finding Gilda, he found the house deserted. He is certain that Gilda was abducted, but he has no idea who the perpetrators were. He is torn between rage that anyone should have dared to cross him, and his pity for the young woman whom he now claims has awakened in him — for the first time — genuine feelings of affection. The Duke expresses a heretofore unrevealed sense of sincerity and compassion for his lost love.

"Parmi veder le lagrime"

Par - mi   veder le   la - grime   scorren - ti   da   quel cig-lio,
I seem to see tears running from those eyes,

Marullo, Ceprano, Borsa, and other courtiers enter the drawing room and gleefully — and heartlessly — narrate their adventures of the previous night, cynically describing Rigoletto's unwitting collaboration as they abducted the young woman they believed was Rigoletto's mistress. The Duke realizes that they are referring to none other than Gilda, and he becomes delighted when he learns that the courtiers have brought her to the palace. He dashes off to the conquest, intending to console his new love who is awaiting him.

The grief-stricken Rigoletto enters the salon, self-controlled, pretending nonchalance, and cynical as he tries to conceal his distress and anxiety. The courtiers greet him with ironical good humor and mock him. In a pathetic spectacle, Rigoletto searches for clues to the whereabouts of his daughter, quickly snatching up a handkerchief from the table in the hope that it may belong to Gilda.

Certain that Gilda is with the Duke and in the palace, he tries to enter the Duke's quarters, but the courtiers bar his way, telling him that the Duke is asleep and cannot be disturbed. But then a page announces that the Duchess wishes to speak to her husband. The courtiers pretend that the Duke has gone hunting, but Rigoletto pierces through the veil of their charade and intuitively senses the truth: he concludes that Gilda is in the palace.

Behind a laughing exterior, Rigoletto continues his search for Gilda. The courtiers mock him, telling him to look for his "mistress" somewhere else. In a fury, Rigoletto astonishes them by revealing the truth, crying out: "Io vo' mia figlia" ("I want my daughter.")

Alternating between threats and pleas — and even attempted force — to enter the Duke's quarters, Rigoletto vents his fury and frustration by violently denouncing the courtiers, simultaneously lashing out at their cruelty with pleas for mercy.

"Cortigiani vil razza, dannata"

Andante mosso agitato
RIGOLETTO

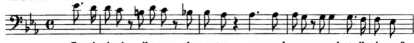

Cor-ti -giani, vil razza da-nnata, per qual prezzo vendeste il mio cor?
Courtiers, damned vile race, for what price have you sold my treasure?

Suddenly, the freshly ravished Gilda emerges from the Duke's apartments and throws herself into her father's arms. Rigoletto's first reaction is one of relief, convincing himself that she is safe, and that perhaps it was all a joke.

Gilda sees her father for the first time in his jester's costume, and each, in a shocking moment of revelation, realizes their shame. Gilda's tears convince Rigoletto that the events that have occurred are more serious. Gilda makes a request to her father: "I want to blush before you, alone." Rigoletto dismisses the courtiers.

Gilda confesses everything that had happened, sadly admitting her guilt. She relates how a young student she had seen in church followed her home, and how she later fell in love with him. When she was abducted and brought to the palace, she was surprised to find that the Duke himself was that young man: in her innocence, she had fallen in love with him, and then abandoned herself to him consensually.

"Tutte le feste al tempio"

Andantino
GILDA

Tutte le fe - ste al tem - pio mentre prega - va Id - dio,
At the festivals at church, while I was praying to God,

During Gilda's poignant exposition, Rigoletto tenderly attempts to comfort his distraught daughter. But he is confused, and refuses to believe what she has told him; Rigoletto is in denial. While under guard, Monterone passes by on his way to prison. He pauses to vent his outrage and anger at a portrait of the Duke: "So, my curse has been in vain, neither a thunderbolt or steel has entered your breast. Duke, you still live happily!"

As Monterone is led away, Rigoletto calls to him, assuring him that they will both be avenged. Rigoletto becomes transformed into a savage fury. He swears a frightful vengeance against the Duke, while Gilda begs in vain that he forgive the man she deeply loves.

"Si vendetta tremenda vendetta"

Allegro vivo
RIGOLETTO

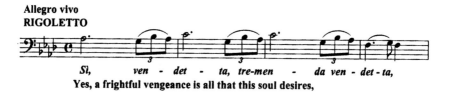

Si,   ven - det - ta, tre-men - da ven - det - ta,
Yes, a frightful vengeance is all that this soul desires,

Act III: Sparafucile's Inn on the deserted banks of the Mincio River

Sparafucile sits inside the Inn, polishing his belt. Outside, Rigoletto and Gilda watch through a small opening in the wall (or window.)

Still full of romantic protestations, Gilda persists that she passionately loves the Duke, and that she truly believes he will return her love. But Rigoletto believes he can cure her affectation for this licentious libertine by bringing her to Sparafucile's Inn; he well knows that what she will witness inside will prove to her that her lover is a capricious, worthless profligate.

The Duke, disguised as a cavalier, is inside the Inn, ordering wine and a room for the night. Gilda now hears her lover in his true character, the libertine Duke advancing his cynical, chauvinist philosophy about the fickleness and capriciousness of women.

"La donna é mobile"

Allegretto
DUKE

La donna è mobile qual piuma al vento, muta d'ac-cen - to e di pen-si -e- ro,
All women are capricious, like a plume in the wind, changing their thoughts,

Sparafucile's sister, Maddalena, a gypsy enchantress, had lured the Duke to the Inn. She now joins her prey. Gilda and Rigoletto remain outside and watch incredulously as the Duke attempts to seduce Maddalena.

The Quartet begins with "Bella figlia dell'amore" ("Pretty daughter of love.") The individual passions of each character stands out in high relief: outside the Inn, Rigoletto repeats his obsession for revenge against the Duke, while Gilda naively expresse her love for him and her willingness to forgive him; inside the Inn, Maddalena half-heartedly repels the Duke's advances, but the Duke pulsates with amorous passion, prepared to offer her anything, even marriage, to succeed in his amorous conquest.

Concealed in the darkness outside, Gilda witnesses the amorous interplay between the Duke and Maddalena, slowly becoming heartbroken and grim as she witnesses how lightly he speaks of love.

Quartet: "Bella figlia dell'amore"

Bel- la figlia del-l'a - mo - re,   schiavo son de'vezzi   tuo - i,
Beautiful daughter of love, I am a slave to your charms,

Rigoletto persuades the disillusioned and heartbroken Gilda to return home, change into male attire, and set out for Verona where he will meet her the next day.

After Gilda leaves, Rigoletto summons Sparafucile and hands over half the assassin's fee to murder the Duke; he promises to pay the remainder when the body is delivered to him in a sack at midnight. Sparafucile offers to throw the body in the river himself, but Rigoletto wants personal satisfaction, insisting that he will return at midnight for the body.

Sparafucile curiously asks Rigoletto the victim's name, and Rigoletto antagonistically replies: "Voui saper anche il mio? Egli è Delitto, Punizion son io" ("Do you want to know my name as well? He is Crime, and mine is Punishment.")

Meanwhile, inside the Inn, the flirtations between Maddalena and the Duke grow more intimate. A storm has gathered, forcing the Duke to stay the night at the Inn.

Gilda has returned and overhears Maddalena and Sparafucile discuss their forthcoming plan to murder the Duke. Maddalena reveals that she has fallen in love with the young cavalier, seduced by his charms. She attempts to dissuade her brother from murdering her new-found love, but Sparafucile fails to understand his sister's sudden sentiment; after all, their only concern is the twenty crowns they will receive for performing the deed.

Maddalena suggests to her brother that he kill the hunchback instead of the man she now endearingly refers to as her "Apollo." Citing his honor, Sparafucile refuses to betray his employer: one does not murder his own client. Maddalena's tears touch Sparafucile and he offers his sister a compromise: if another stranger should chance to call at the Inn before midnight, the hour of Rigoletto's return, he will become the murder victim. In either case, the hunchback will still receive a corpse for his money. But if no one appears, Maddalena's new love must die.

Gilda has overheard Maddalena and Sparafucile discuss their sinister murder plans, a choice of death for Gilda's lover, or their client, her father Rigoletto. Gilda fears for her lover's life and resolves to sacrifice her own life for him; with conviction and determination, she decides that she will be the next person to enter the Inn.

Lightning and thunder crack as the storm increases with sudden and overwhelming fury. Gilda summons up her courage, knocks on the door, and calls out: "Have pity on a beggar who wants shelter for the night." As the door opers, she pathetically exclaims, "God forgive them." Gilda enters the Inn, and is immediately stabbed by Sparafucile's sword.

The storm becomes more violent, and then subsides. All is silent.

As midnight strikes, Rigoletto returns to the Inn. Sparafucile delivers the sack containing the dead victim. He offers to throw the sack in the river, but Rigoletto claims his privilege and satisfaction; he wants to savor the triumph of his vengeance.

The gloating Rigoletto drags the sack toward the river. In his moment of victory, he proclaims:

"Ora mi guarda o mondo! Quest'è un buffone, ed un potente è questo! Ei sta sotto i miei piedi! È desso! Oh gioia!"

("World look at me now! Here is a buffoon, and a powerful buffoon! And standing under my foot, it is him! Oh joy!")

Rigoletto trembles when he hears the Duke's voice in the distance: "La donna é mobile." In disbelief, he cries out that it must be a dream or an illusion. But if not, who is in the sack? It is pitch dark with occasional lightning providing the only visibility. Rigoletto tears the sack open, and a sudden flash of lightning reveals Gilda's face. He cannot believe his senses, but the faint voice from the sack reveals that it is indeed his beloved Gilda.

Gilda is dying from her wounds, but with her last breath, she begs Rigoletto to forgive the Duke, and also to forgive her, explaining that she indeed loved him so much.

"V'ho ingannato"

Andante
GILDA

V'ho ingannato colpevole fu - i   l'amai troppo ora muoio per lu - i!
I have deceived you. I was guilty. I loved him too much. Now I die for him!

In a touching farewell, "Lassù in ciel" ("Up there in Heaven"), Gilda pours out her love for her father, assuring him that she will be united with her mother in Heaven, where they will both pray for him.

"Lassù in ciel"

Andante
GILDA

Lassù in cielo, vi - ci-no al -la madre,   in   e -   terno per voi preghiero,
Up there, in Heaven, near my mother, I will forever pray for you,

Rigoletto cries out, "She is dead." His screams reveal the utter futility of this tragic moment of fury and frustration, his explanation for the collapse of his world uttered in his last words: "Ah! La maledizione" ("Ah, the curse.")

Monterone's curse has been fulfilled: Gilda's death overcomes Rigoletto with disaster and despair; he has become a victim of his own evil.

RIGOLETTO

Libretto

Act I - Scene 1

A magnificent and sumptuous hall in the palace of the Duke of Mantua.
Ladies, gentlemen, and pages pass through the hall. Others dance in the inner rooms.
The Duke and the courtier Borsa are deep in conversation.

Duke:
Della mia bella incognita borghese
toccare il fin dell'avventura io voglio.

Borsa:
Di quella giovin che vedete al tempio?

Duca:
Da tre mesi ogni festa.

Borsa:
La sua dimora?

Duca:
In un remoto calle; misterioso un uom
v'entra ogni notte.

Borsa:
E sa colei chi sia l'amante suo?

Duca:
Lo ignora.

Duke:
I'll soon succeed in my adventure with
that unknown woman.

Borsa:
Is it that young woman you saw in
church?

Duke:
I've been following her every Sunday for
three months.

Borsa:
Where does she live?

Duke:
In an obscure street; a strange man enters
the house every night.

Borsa:
Does she know that you want to be her
lover?

Duke:
She's unaware of my intentions.

A group of ladies and gentlemen pass before the Duke and Borsa.

Borsa:
Quante beltà! Mirate.

Duca:
Le vince tutte di Cepran la sposa.

Borsa:
What beauty! Look at them.

Duke:
Ceprano's wife is the most beautiful.

Borsa:
Non v'oda il conte, o Duca.

Duca:
A me che importa?

Borsa:
Dirlo ad altra ei potria.

Duca:
Né sventura per me certo saria.

Borsa: *(aside to the Duke)*
Duke, don't let her husband hear you.

Duke:
Why should I care?

Borsa:
He might tell another woman.

Duke:
It wouldn't be a misfortune for me.

Allegretto
DUKE

Questa o quella   *per me pari so- no a quant'altre d'intor - no,*

Questa o quella per me pari sono a
quant'altre d'intorno, d'intorno mi vedo;
del mio core l'impero non cedo meglio ad
una che ad altra beltà.

This woman or that woman, they're all
the same. I'm surrounded by so many.
My heart never ceases to want to conquer
one beauty or another.

La costoro avvenenza è qual dono di che
il fato ne infiora la vita; s'oggi questa mi
torna gradita, forse un'altra, forse un'altra
doman lo sarà, un'altra, forse un'altra
doman lo sarà.

Love is a gift, a fate that embellishes and
invigorates life; if today this one is
disagreeable, perhaps another, perhaps it
will be another tomorrow, perhaps there
will be another tomorrow.

La costanza, tiranna del core, detestiamo
qual morbo, qual morbo crudele;
sol chi vuole si serbe fidele; non v'ha
amor, se non v'è libertà.

Fidelity is a cruel disease, a tyranny of
the heart, and a disease we detest;
if one wants to be faithful, there is no
love, and there is no freedom.

De' mariti il geloso furore, degli amanti le
smanie derido; anco d'Argo i cent'occhi
disfido se mi punge, se mi punge una
qualche beltà, se mi punge una qualche
beltà.

I mock marital jealousies with a fury;
I challenge the hundred eyes of Argus
because if a woman stings me, she stings
me with some of her beauty.

Ladies and gentlemen dance a Minuet.
The Countess Ceprano passes before the Duke, and he addresses her gallantly.

Duca:
Partite? Crudele!

Duke: *(to the Countess)*
Are you leaving? How cruel of you!

Contesa de Ceprano:
Seguire lo sposo m'è forza a Ceprano.

Countess Ceprano:
It is my duty to follow my husband.

Duca:
Ma dee luminoso in Corte tal astro qual
sole brillare. Per voi qui ciascuno dovrà
palpitare. Per voi già possente la fiamma
d'amore, inebria, conquide, distrugge il
mio core.

Duke:
You are the most radiant of all the
beauties of the Court. My heart throbs to
possess you. The flame of love has
intoxicated me and conquered my heart.

The Duke fervently kisses the Countess's hand.

Contessa di Ceprano:
Calmatevi.

Countess Ceprano:
Calm yourself.

Duca:
La fiamma d'amore inebria, conquide,
distrugge il mio core.

Duke:
The flame of love has intoxicated me and
conquered my heart.

Contessa di Ceprano:
Calmatevi, calmatevi.

Countess Ceprano:
Calm yourself. Calm yourself.

Duca:
Per voi già possente la fiamma d'amore
inebria, conquide, distrugge il mio core.

Duke:
To possess you, the flame of love has
intoxicated me and conquered my heart.

The Duke offers his arm to the Countess. As both leave, Rigoletto enters.

Rigoletto:
In testa che avete, signor di Ceprano?

Rigoletto: *(sarcastically to Ceprano)*
What disturbs you, lord Ceprano?

Ceprano gestures that he is agitated. He follows the Duke and the Countess.

Rigoletto:
Ei sbuffa! Vedete?

Rigoletto: *(to the courtiers)*
He's fuming! Did you see him?

Cortigiani:
Che festa!

Courtiers:
What amusement!

Rigoletto:
Oh sì!

Rigoletto:
Oh indeed!

Borsa:
Il Duca qui pur si diverte!

Borsa:
The Duke indeed finds pleasures here!

Rigoletto:
Così non è sempre?
Che nuove scoperte!
Il giuoco ed il vino, le feste, la danza,
battaglie, conviti, ben tutto gli sta.

Or della Contessa l'assedio egli avanza, e
intanto il marito fremendo ne va.

Rigoletto:
And when isn't it that way?
What new adventures he discovers!
Wherever he goes, there's always games,
wine, amusement, the dance,
battles, banquets.
Now he advances and seizes the
Countess, and the cuckolded husband is
trembling from his misfortune.

Cynically laughing, Rigoletto departs. Marullo enters eagerly.

Marullo:
Gran nuova! Gran nuova!

Marullo:
I've great news! Great news!

Borsa:
Che avvenne? Parlate!

Borsa:
What happened? Tell us?

Marullo:
Stupir ne dovrete.

Marullo:
You'll be astonished.

Borsa:
Narrate, narrate!

Borsa:
Tell us, tell us!

Marullo:
Ah, ah! Rigoletto.

Marullo: *(laughing)*
Ha, ha! It's about Rigoletto.

Borsa:
Ebben?

Borsa:
Well?

Marullo:
Caso enorme!

Marullo:
It's incredible!

Borsa:
Perduto ha la gobba?
Non è più difforme?

Borsa:
Has he lost his hunchback?
He's no longer deformed?

Marullo:
Più strana è la cosa!
Il pazzo possiede....

Marullo: *(very seriously)*
The truth is even stranger!
The crazy fool has....

Borsa:
Infine?

Borsa:
Treasures?

Marullo:
Un'amante!

Borsa:
Un'amante! Chi il crede?

Marullo:
Il gobbo in Cupido or s'è trasformato.

Borsa:
Quel mostro? Cupido!

Borsa, Marullo:
Cupido beato!

Marullo:
He has a lover!

Borsa: *(surprised)*
A lover! Who would believe that?

Marullo:
The hunchback has become Cupid.

Borsa:
Isn't he a monster? Cupid!

Borsa, Marullo:
A blessed Cupid!

The Duke returns, followed by Rigoletto, and then Ceprano.
The Duke addresses Rigoletto.

Duca:
Ah, più di Ceprano importuno non v'è.
La cara sua sposa è un angiol per me!

Rigoletto:
Rapitela.

Duca:
È detto; ma il farlo?

Rigoletto:
Sta sera.

Duca:
Non pensi tu al conte?

Rigoletto:
Non c'è la prigione?

Duca:
Ah no.

Rigoletto:
Ebben, s'esilia.

Duca:
Nemmeno, buffone.

Duke:
Ceprano's presence here annoys me.
His dear wife is an angel for me!

Rigoletto:
Abduct her.

Duke:
That's easy to say; but how can I do it?

Rigoletto:
Do it tonight.

Duke:
What about her husband?

Rigoletto:
What about prison?

Duke:
Oh, no.

Rigoletto:
Well, exile him.

Duke:
Never, that's ridiculous.

Rigoletto:
Allora, allora la testa.

Rigoletto: (gesturing decapitation)
Then, then his head.

Conte di Ceprano:
(Oh l'anima nera!)

Count Ceprano: (aside)
(What an evil soul!)

Duca:
Che dì, questa testa?

Duke: (tapping the Count's shoulder)
Will your head yield easily?

Rigoletto:
È ben naturale! Che far di tal testa?
A cosa ella vale?

Rigoletto:
Naturally! What to do with that head?
Will she appreciate it?

Conte di Ceprano:
Marrano!

Count Ceprano: (grasping his sword)
You devil!

Duca:
Fermate!

Duke: (to Ceprano)
Stop!

Rigoletto:
Da rider mi fa.

Rigoletto: *(to Ceprano)*
You're making me laugh.

Marullo:
In furia è montato!

Marullo: *(discussing Ceprano)*
His anger is mounting!

Duca:
Buffone, vien qua.

Duke: (to Rigoletto)
Jester, come here.

Borsa:
In furia è montato!

Borsa:
His anger is mounting!

Marullo:
In furia è montato!

Marullo:
His anger is mounting!

Cortigiani:
In furia è montato!

Courtiers:
His anger is mounting!

Duca:
Ah sempre tu spingi lo scherzo
all'estremo.

Duke: (to Rigoletto)
You always push your joking to extremes.

Conte di Ceprano:
Vendetta del pazzo!Contr'esso un rancore
di noi chi non ha?

Count Ceprano: (to the courtiers)
A merciless revenge! Who among you
hasn't been the victim of his vindictiveness?

Rigoletto:
Che coglier mi puote?
Di loro non temo.

Duca:
Quell'ira che sfidi, colpir ti potrà.

Conte di Ceprano:
Vendetta! In armi chi ha core.

Borsa, Marullo:
Ma come?

Rigoletto:
Del duca il protetto nessun toccherà.

Conte di Ceprano:
Doman sia da me. A notte.

Borsa, Marullo:
Sì. Sarà.

Duca:
Ah sempre tu spingi....

Rigoletto:
Che coglier mi puote?
Di loro non temo.

Borsa, Marulla, Conte di Ceprano:
Vendetta del pazzo! Contr'esso un rancore

Duca:
Lo scherzo all'estremo....

Rigoletto:
Del duca il protetto nessun toccherà, no, no....

Borsa, Marullo, Conte di Ceprano:
Pei tristi suoi modi di noi chi non ha?

Rigoletto:
What is this gathering planning for me?
I don't fear them.

Duke:
The anger you have aroused will strike back at you.

Count Ceprano:
Vengeance! And with arms if you have the courage.

Borsa, Marullo:
But how?

Rigoletto:
I am protected by the Duke, and no one can touch me.

Count Ceprano:
Tomorrow join me. At night.

Borsa, Marullo:
Yes. We'll be there.

Duke:
You always push too much....

Rigoletto:
What is this gathering planning for me?
I don't fear them.

Borsa, Marullo, Count Ceprano:
A merciless revenge! Who among you hasn't been the victim of his vindictiveness?

Duke:
The excessive joking....

Rigoletto:
I am protected by the Duke, and no one can touch me, no, no.....

Borsa, Marullo, Count Ceprano:
Who among you hasn't been the victim of his vindictiveness?

Duca:
Ah sempre tu spingi lo scherzo
all'estremo....

Duke:
You always push your joking to
extremes....

Rigoletto:
Nessun, nessuno, nessun, nessuno.

Rigoletto:
No, one, no one, no one, no one.

Conte di Ceprano:
Vendetta! Vendetta!

Count Ceprano:
Vengeance! Vengeance!

Borsa, Marullo:
Vendetta! Vendetta!

Borsa:
Vengeance! Vengeance!

Duca:
Quell'ira che sfidi, quell'ira che sfidi,
colpir ti potrà.

Duke:
The anger you have aroused will strike
back at you.

Rigoletto:
nessun, nessuno del duca il protetto,
nessuno toccherà.

Rigoletto:
No one, no one, I am protected by the
Duke, and no one can touch me.

Conte di Ceprano:
Vendetta! Sta notte chi ha core sia in armi
da me.

Count Ceprano:
Vengeance! Tonight those who have
courage bear arms with me.

Borsa, Marullo:
Vendetta! Sì! A notte sarà.

Borsa, Marullo:
Vengeance! Yes, It will be tonight!

Duca:
Ah sempre tu spingi....

Duke:
You always push too much....

Rigoletto:
Che coglier mi puote?
Di loro non temo....

Rigoletto:
What is this gathering planning for me?
I don't fear them....

Borsa, Marullo, Conte di Ceprano:
Vendetta del pazzo! Contr'esso un
rancore....

Borsa, Marullo, Count Ceprano:
A merciless revenge! Who among you
hasn't been the victim....

Duca:
Lo scherzo all'estremo....

Duke:
The joking is excessive....

Rigoletto:
Del duca il protetto nessun toccherà, no,
no....

Rigoletto:
I am protected by the Duke, and no one
can touch me, no, no.....

Borsa, Marullo Conte di Ceprano::
pei tristi suoi modi di noi chi non ha?

Borsa, Marullo, Count Ceprano:
Who among you hasn't been the victim
of his vindictiveness?

Duca:
Ah sempre tu spingi lo scherzo
all'estremo....

Duke:
You always push your joking to
extremes....

Rigoletto:
Nessun, nessuno, nessun, nessuno.

Rigoletto:
No one, no one, no one, no one.
woe

Borsa, Marullo, Conte di Ceprano:
Vendetta! Vendetta!

Borsa, Marullo, Count Ceprano:
Vengeance! Vengeance!

Duca:
Quell'ira che sfidi, quell'ira che sfidi,
colpir ti potrà.

Duke:
The anger you have aroused will strike
back at you.

Rigoletto:
Nessun, nessuno del duca il protetto,
nessuno toccherà.

Rigoletto:
No one, I am protected by the Duke, and
no one can touch me.

Conte di Ceprano:
Vendetta! Sta notte chi ha core sia in armi
da me.

Count Ceprano:
Vengeance! Tonight those who have
courage bear arms with me.

Borsa, Marullo:
Vendetta! Sì! A notte sarà.

Borsa, Marullo:
Vengeance! Yes! It will be tonight.

Borsa, Marullo, Conte di Ceprano:
Sì vendetta!

Borsa, Marullo, Count Ceprano:
Yes vengeance!

Dancers from the other rooms enter the hall.

Duca, Rigoletto:
Tutto è gioja!

Duke, Rigoletto:
What entertainment!

Borsa, Marullo, Conte di Ceprano:
Sì vendetta! Sì, vendetta!
Sì, vendetta!

Borsa, Marullo, Count Ceprano:
Yes vengeance! Yes vengeance!
Yes vengeance!

Duca, Rigoletto:
Tutto è festa!

Duke, Rigoletto:
What entertainment!

Tutti:
Tutto è gioja, tutto è festa; tutto invitaci a godere!
Oh guardate, non par questa or la reggia del piacere!

All:
So much entertainment and amusement; all the guests are enjoying themselves!
Look, nothing equals the extent of this pleasure!

The voice of Count Monterone is heard from outside.

Monterone:
Ch'io gli parli.

Monterone:
I demand to speak to him.

Duca:
No!

Duke:
No!

Monterone:
Il voglio.

Monterone: *(as he enters)*
I demand it.

Borsa, Rigoletto, Marullo, Ceprano:
Monterone!

Borsa, Rigoletto, Marullo, Ceprano:
Monterone!

Monterone:
Sì, Monteron, la voce mia qual tuono vi scuoterà dovunque.

Monterone: *(staring at the Duke)*
Yes, Monterone, the voice that makes you shudder.

Rigoletto:
Ch'io gli parli.
Voi congiuraste, voi congiuraste contro noi, signore; e noi, e noi, clementi in vero, perdonammo
Qual vi piglia or delirio, a tutte l'ore di vostra figlia a reclamar l'onore?

Rigoletto: *(mimicking Monterone)*
I demand to speak to him.
You have conspired, you have conspired against us. And we, and we forgive you with compassionate clemency.
What's the matter, are you still obsessed to reclaim your daughter's honor?

Monterone:
Novello insulto!

Monterone: *(with contemptuous anger)*
Another insult!

Ah sì, a turbare, ah sì, a turbare sarò vostr'orgie, verrò a gridare fino a che vegga restarsi inulto di mia famiglia l'atroce insulto; e se al carnefice pur mi darete. spettro terribile mi rivedrete, portante in mano il teschio mio, vendetta a chiedere, vendetta a chiedere al mondo, al mondo, a Dio.

Yes, I am tormented, tormented by your debauchery. I have come to condemn the atrocious insults you have perpetrated against my family; and if you send me to the executioner, my head will haunt you like a horrible ghost. I ask for the world to avenge me, and I ask vengeance from God.

Duca:
Non più, arrestatelo!

Duke:
That's enough, arrest him!

Rigoletto:
È matto!

Borsa, Marullo, Conte di Ceprano:
Quai detti!

Monterone:
Ah, siate entrambi voi maledetti!

Slanciare il cane a leon morente è vile, o
Duca.

E tu, serpente, tu che d'un padre ridi al
dolore, sii maledetto!

Rigoletto:
(Che sento! Orrore!)

Duke, Borsa, Marullo, Ceprano:
Oh tu che la festa audace hai turbato, da
un genio d'inferno qui fosti guidato.

Rigoletto:
(Orrore!)

Duke, Borsa, Marullo, Ceprano:
È vano ogni detto, di qua t'allontana va,
trema, o vegliardo, dell'ira sovranna è
vano ogni detto, di qua t'allontana va,
trema, o vegliardo, dell'ira sovrana tu
l'hai provocata, più speme non v'è,
un'ora fatale fu questa per te, un'ora
fatale fu questa per te, fu questa per te.

Rigoletto:
He's mad!

Borsa, Marullo, Count Ceprano:
What impudence!

Monterone: *(to the Duke and Rigoletto)*
I curse both of you!

Duke, it is unconscionable to unleash this
vile dog at a dying lion.
(to Rigoletto)
And you, serpent, who mock a father's
agony, be accursed!

Rigoletto: *(stricken by terror)*
(What do I hear! What a horror!

Duke, Borsa, Marullo, Ceprano:
You have disturbed our amusement, your
audacious game has led us to Hell.

Rigoletto:
(What a horror!)

Duke, Borsa, Marullo, Ceprano:
Your words are hopeless. The curse
cannot be removed. Tremble, old man,
you have provoked the indignation of the
most holy.
There is no hope for you, a fatal destiny
has been ordained for you.

Monterone is led away by guards.
Rigoletto leaves in panic and terror.

Act I - Scene 2

A dark, deserted street at night.
There is a humble house with a small courtyard surrounded by a wall.
In the courtyard of the house there is a large tree and a garden seat.
In the wall a door leads to the street, and above the wall, a terrace supported by arches.
A door from the first floor opens to a terrace, from which there is a staircase.
From one side, the Ceprano palace is visible in the distance.

Rigoletto approaches his house, completely disguised by his cloak.
He is followed by a stranger: he is Sparafucile, an ominous looking man, wrapped in a
cloak from which the hilt of a sword projects.

Rigoletto:
(Quel vecchio maledivami!)

Rigoletto: *(muttering to himself)*
(That old man cursed me!

Andante mosso

Sparafucile:
Signor!

Sparafucile: *(nearing Rigoletto)*
Sir!

Rigoletto:
Va, non ho niente.

Rigoletto:
Go away, I have nothing.

Sparafucile:
Né il chiesi. A voi presente un uom di
spada sta.

Sparafucile:
That is not my reason. I present myself to
you as a man of the sword.

Rigoletto:
Un ladro?

Rigoletto:
A robber?

Sparafucile:
Un uom che libera per poco da un rivale,
e voi ne avete.

Sparafucile: *(mysteriously)*
A man who for very little money can rid
you of a rival, if you have the need.

Rigoletto:
Quale?

Rigoletto:
How?

Sparafucile:
La vostra donna è là.

Sparafucile:
Your woman is in there.

Rigolettto:
(Che sento!)
E quanto spendere per un signor dovrei?

Rigoletto:
(He knows my secret!)
How much does it cost to slay a noble?

Sparafucile:
Prezzo maggior vorrei.

Sparafucile:
I ask a high price for that.

Rigoletto:
Com'usasi pagar?

Rigoletto:
When must the price be paid?

Sparafucile:
Una metà s'anticipa, il resto si dà poi.

Sparafucile:
One half beforehand, the rest after the deed.

Rigoletto:
(Dimonio!)
E come puoi tanto securo oprar?

Rigoletto:
(What a demon!)
How sure are you of success?

Sparafucile:
Soglio in cittade uccidere, oppure nel mio tetto. L'uomo di sera aspetto, una stoccata, e muor.

Sparafucile:
I use my house, because it is dangerous to kill in the city. I await the victim in the evening; one thrust, and he is dead.

Rigoletto:
E come in casa?

Rigoletto:
How do you lure them to your house?

Sparafucile:
È facile, m'aiuta mia sorella, per le vie danza è bella. Chi voglio attira, e allor.

Sparafucile:
It is easy. My sister helps me. She lures them with her beauty and by dancing.

Rigoletto:
Comprendo.

Rigoletto:
I understand.

Sparafucile:
Senza strepito. È questo il mio stromento. Vi serve?

Sparafucile: *(showing his sword)*
There is no noise. This is my instrument. Can it serve you?

Rigoletto:
No, al momento.

Rigoletto:
No, not at the moment.

Sparafucile:
Peggio per voi.

Sparafucile:
You may regret it.

Rigoletto:
Chi sa?

Rigoletto:
Who knows?

Sparafucile:
Sparafucil mi nomino.

Sparafucile:
My name is Sparafucil.

Rigoletto:
Straniero?

Rigoletto:
A foreigner?

Sparafucile:
Borgognone.

Sparafucile: *(begins to depart)*
From Borgognone.

Rigoletto:
E dove all'occasione?

Rigoletto:
If I need you, where can I find you?

Sparafucile:
Qui sempre a sera.

Sparafucile:
Here, every evening.

Rigoletto:
Va.

Rigoletto:
Go away.

Sparafucile:
Sparafucil, Sparafucil.

Sparafucile: *(as he departs)*
Sparafucil, Sparafucil.

Rigoletto looks after Sparafucile intently.

Adagio
RIGOLETTO

Pa - ri   sia - mo!   io   la lin - gua,   egli ha il pugna - le.

Rigoletto:
Pari siamo! Io la lingua, egli ha il pugnale;
l'uomo son io che ride, ei quel che
spegne!
Quel vecchio maledivami!
O uomini! O natura!
Vil scellerato mi faceste voi!
Oh rabbia! Esser difforme!
Esser buffone!

Non dover, non poter altro che ridere!
Il retaggio d'ogni uom m'è tolto, il pianto!

Rigoletto:
We are the same! I use my tongue, he
uses the dagger; I am the man who
ridicules, and he is the one who kills!
That old man cursed me!
Oh world! Oh nature!
You made me wicked and evil!
What a fate! To be deformed!
To be a jester!

I am commanded to make others laugh!
I have inherited everyone's sorrows and
tears!

Questo padrone mio, giovin, giocondo, sì possente, bello, sonnecchiando mi dice: fa ch'io rida, buffone, forzarmi deggio, e farlo!	My master, young, handsome, rich and powerful, even commands me in his sleep: Make me laugh, jester, and I must force myself to obey him!
O, dannazione! Odio a voi, cortigiani schernitori! Quanta in mordervi ho gioia! Se iniquo son, per cagion vostra è solo. Ma in altr'uom qui mi cangio!	Oh damnation! I hate you, contemptible courtiers! My only joy is to taunt you! If I am vile, it is because of you. But in this house I am different!
Quel vecchio malediami! Tal pensiero perché conturba ognor la mente mia? Mi coglierà sventura? Ah no, è follia!	That old man cursed me! Why does that thought keep agitating my mind? Is it an evil omen? No, it is mere folly!

Rigoletto open the gate with a key, and then enters the courtyard.
Gilda rushes from the house and throws herself into her father's arms.

Allegro vivo

Rigoletto:
Figlia!

Rigoletto:
My daughter!

Gilda:
Mio padre!

Gilda:
My father!

Rigoletto:
A te dappresso trova sol gioia il core oppresso.

Rigoletto:
To be near to you is my only joy; you soothe my grieving heart.

Gilda:
Oh quanto amore!

Gilda:
Oh, you love me so much!

Rigoletto:
Mia vita sei! Senza te in terra qual bene avrei?

Rigoletto:
You are my life! Without you, what would I have in the world?

Gilda:
Voi sospirate! Che v'ange tanto?
Lo dite a questa povera figlia.
Se v'ha mistero per lei sia franto.
Ch'ella conosca la sua famiglia.

Gilda:
You are sighing! What troubles you?
Tell your poor daughter.
If something bothers you,
share it with you daughter.

Rigoletto:
Tu non ne hai.

Rigoletto:
You wouldn't understand it.

Gilda:
Qual nome avete?

Gilda:
What is your name?

Rigoletto:
A te che importa?

Rigoletto:
Is it that important to you?

Gilda:
Se non volete di voi parlarmi.

Gilda:
You don't wish to tell me.

Rigoletto:
Non uscir mai.

Rigoletto: *(interrupting Gilda)*
Don't ever leave the house.

Gilda:
Non vo' che al tempio.

Gilda:
Not even to go to church.

Rigoletto:
Or ben tu fai.

Rigoletto:
That is all right.

Gilda:
Se non di voi, almen chi sia fate ch'io
sappia la madre mia.

Gilda:
Perhaps at least you can tell me about my
mother.

Andante
RIGOLETTO

Deh non parla-re al mi-se-ro   del suo   perdu-to   be   -   ne.

Rigoletto:
Deh non parlare al misero del suo perduto
bene
Ella sentia, quell'angelo, pietà delle mie
pene.
Solo, difforme, povero, per compassion
mi amò.
Ah! Moria, moria, le zolle coprano lievi
quel capo amato.
Sola or tu resti al misero.
Dio, sii ringraziato!

Rigoletto:
Don't speak of my grief since I lost that
love.
That angel felt pity for my anguish and
sorrows.
She loved me compassionately, a man
who was alone, deformed, and poor.
She is dead, covered by earth, her soul
raised to Heaven.
Only you remain from that sorrow.
God, may I thank you for that!

Gilda:
Quanto dolor!
Che spremere sì amaro pianto può?
Padre, non più, calmatevi.
Mi lacera tal vista.
Il nome vostro ditemi, il duol che sì
v'attrista.

Rigoletto:
A che nomarmi? È inutile!
Padre ti sono, e basti.
Me forse al mondo temono, d'alcuno ho
forse gli asti.
Altri mi maledicono.

Gilda:
Patria, parenti, amici, voi dunque non
avete?

Rigoletto:
Patria! Parenti! Dici?
Culto, famiglia, patria, il mio universo è
in te!

Gilda:
Ah se può lieto rendervi, gioia è la vita a
me!

Già da tre lune son qui venuta, né la
cittade ho ancor veduta; se il concedete,
farlo or potrei.

Rigoletto:
Mai, Mai! Uscita, dimmi unqua sei?

Gilda:
No.

Rigoletto:
Guai!

Gilda:
(Ah! Che dissi!)

Gilda: *(sobbing)*
What suffering!
How that love has moved you to tears?
Father, no more, calm yourself.
Your look upsets me.
Tell me your name, and the distress that
has saddened you.

Rigoletto:
What is my name? It is unnecessary!
I am father, and that is enough.
In the world, there are some who fear me,
and some who hate me.
Others curse me.

Gilda:
Then you do not have a homeland,
relatives, or friends?

Rigoletto:
Homeland! Relatives! What do you say?
My soul, family, country, my entire
universe is you!

Gilda:
Whatever makes you happy, gives me joy
and happiness!

But we've already here three months, and
I haven't seen the city yet. I'd like to be
able to, if you would let me.

Rigoletto:
Never, never! Have you gone out?

Gilda:
No.

Rigoletto:
It would be disastrous!

Gilda:
(Oh, what I have said!)

Rigoletto:
Ben te ne guarda!
(Potrien seguirla, rapirla ancora! Qui d'un
buffone si disonora la figlia, e se ne ride.
Orror!)

Rigoletto:
Obey me!
(They would follow her and rape her, and
laugh as they dishonored the daughter of
a jester. What a horror!)

Rigoletto rushes towards the house and calls Giovanna, Gilda's nurse.

Olà?

Can you come out?

Giovanna:
Signor!

Giovanna:
Sir!

Rigoletto:
Venendo, mi vede alcuno?
Bada, di' il vero.

Rigoletto:
Has anyone seen me coming here?
Tell me the truth.

Giovanna:
Ah no, nessuno.

Giovanna:
No, no one.

Rigoletto:
Sta ben. La porta che dà al bastione è
sempre chiusa?

Rigoletto:
Very well. Has the door from the terrace
always remained closed?

Giovanna:
Ognor si sta.

Giovanna:
Always closed.

Allegro moderato assai
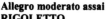
RIGOLETTO

Ah! Veglia o don - na, questo fio-re che a te pur - ro confi- dai.

Rigoletto:
Ah! Veglia, o donna, questo fiore che a te
puro confidai; veglia attenta, e non sia
mai che s'offuschi il suo candor.
Tu dei venti dal furore ch 'altri fiori
hanno piegato lo difendi, e immacolato lo
ridona al genitor.

Rigoletto: *(to Giovanna)*
Lady, guard this innocent flower who I
place in your trust; watch her carefully,
and don't let her purity ever be darkened.
In threatening storms other flowers have
yielded their defense, and returned a
daughter to a father in disgrace.

Gilda:
Quanto affetto! Quali cure!
Che temete, padre mio?

Gilda:
So much love! So much concern!
Father, why are you so fearful?

Lassù in cielo, presso Dio veglia un angiol protettor. Da noi stoglie le sventure di mia madre il priego santo; non fia mai divelto o infranto questo a voi diletto fior.

Up there in Heaven, close to God, is my mother, an angel protecting us from misfortune; she protects your treasured flower.

Meanwhile, the Duke, dressed in ordinary street clothes, appears outside Rigoletto's house.

Rigoletto:
Alcuno è fuori.

Rigoletto: *(hearing noise)*
Someone is out there.

Rigoletto opens the courtyard door and goes out to investigate the noise. The Duke evades him, enters the courtyard, and hides behind a tree. He throws a purse to Giovanna, and makes a sign that she be silent.

Gilda:
Cielo!Sempre novel sospetto.

Gilda:
Heavens! Always new suspicions.

Rigoletto:
Alla chiesa vi seguiva mai nessuno?

Rigoletto: *(questioning Giovanna)*
Did anyone follow you from church?

Giovanna:
Mai.

Giovanna:
No one.

Duca:
(Rigoletto!)

Duke: *(from hiding)*
(Rigoletto!)

Rigoletto:
Se talor qui picchiano guardatevi da aprir.

Rigoletto:
If someone knocks, be cautious in opening the gate.

Giovanna:
Nemmeno al duca.

Giovanna:
Not even for the Duke.

Rigoletto:
Meno che a tutti a lui.
Mia figlia addio.

Rigoletto:
Least of all him.
Farewell my daughter.

Duca:
(Sua figlia!)

Duke:
(His daughter!)

Gilda:
Addio, mio padre.

Gilda:
Farewell, my father.

Rigoletto embraces Gilda, and then departs, carefully closing the door behind him.

Gilda:
Giovanna, ho dei rimorsi.

Gilda:
Giovanna, I feel so guilty.

Giovanna:
E perché mai?

Giovanna:
And why?

Gilda:
Tacqui che un giovin ne seguiva al
tempio.

Gilda:
I didn't tell him that a young man
followed me home from church.

Giovanna:
Perché ciò dirgli?
L'odiate dunque cotesto giovin, voi?

Giovanna:
Why was it necessary to tell him?
Do you want to chase the young man away?

Gilda:
No, no, ché troppo è bello e spira amore.

Gilda:
No, he's so handsome and inspires love.

Giovanna:
E magnanimo sembra e gran signore.

Giovanna:
He seems to be so generous and noble.

Gilda:
Signor né principe, io lo vorrei;
sento che povero, più l'amerei.
Sognando o vigile sempre lo chiamo,
e l'alma in estasi gli dice t'a...

Gilda:
He's not a prince, although I would wish it;
I love him more because he's poor.
I always call him in my dreams,
and my ecstatic soul tells him I love...

The Duke emerges from hiding, signals Giovanna to leave.
Then he kneels before Gilda.

Duca:
T'amo! T'amo ripetilo,
sì caro accento, un puro schiudimi ciel di
contento!

Duke:
I love you! I love you and I repeat it,
a beloved sound, that opens the bliss of
the Heavens!

Gilda:
Giovanna? Ahi misera!
Non v'è più alcuno che qui rispondami!
Oh Dio! Nessuno!

Gilda: *(surprised and fearful)*
Giovanna? How frightful!
There's no one here to answer me!
Oh God! No one!

Duca:
Son io coll'anima che ti rispondo.
Ah due che s'amano son tutto un mondo!

Duke:
It is I whose soul answers you.
Two people who love each other is all
there is in the entire world!

Gilda:
Chi mai, chi giungere vi fece a me?

Gilda:
Who made you come here?

Duca:
Se angelo o demone, che importa a te?
Io t'amo.

Gilda:
Uscitene.

Duca:
Uscire! Adesso!
Ora che accendene un fuoco istesso!
Ah inseparabile d'amore il dio stringeva,
o vergine, tuo fato al mio!

Duke:
Angel or demon, is it important to you?
I love you.

Gilda:
Leave me.

Duke:
Leave! Right now!
Now that the fire has been kindled!
Innocent maiden, we are possessed by an
inseparable love. Your fate is to be mine!

Andantino
DUKE

È il sol dell'anima, la vita è a-more sua vo - ce è il palpito del nos-tro core.

È il sol dell'anima, la vita è amore, sua
voce è il palpito del nostro core.
E fama e gloria, potenza e trono, umane,
fragili qui cose sono:
una pur avvene, sola, divina, é amor che
agli angeli, agli angeli più ne avvicina!

Adunque amiamoci, donna celeste,
d'invidia agli uomini, sarò per te.

Life is love, the sun of the soul, its voice
the throb of our hearts.
Fame and glory, power and throne,
humanity, are unimportant here:
one future, ours, divine, is love that even
the angels cannot approach!

Therefore we love each other, celestial
woman, envy of men, and I will be yours.

Gilda:
Ah de' miei vergini sogni son queste le
voci tenere, sì care a me!

Gilda:
That tender voice is from my sublime
dreams. Yes, you are dear to me!

Duca:
Che m'ami, deh! Ripetimi.

Duke:
Repeat to me that you love me!

Gilda:
L'udiste.

Gilda:
Listen to it.

Duca:
Oh me felice!

Duke:
You make me so happy!

Gilda:
Il nome vostro ditemi; saperlo non mi lice?

Gilda:
Tell me your name. Would I forget it if I knew it?

Ceprano:
(Il loco è qui.)

Ceprano: *(in the street)*
(This is the place.)

Duca:
Mi nomino.

Duke: *(thinking with seriousness)*
My name.

Borsa:
Sta ben.

Borsa: *(to Ceprano)*
Very well.

Duca:
Gualtier Maldè. Studente sono, e povero.

Duke:
Walter Maldè. I am a poor student.

Giovanna:
Rumor di passi è fuore.

Giovanna: *(returning in agitation)*
There's the noise of footsteps outside.

Gilda:
Forse mio padre.

Gilda:
Perhaps it is my father.

Duca:
(Ah cogliere potessi il traditore che sì mi sturba!)

Duke:
(If I could only find the traitor who has thwarted my adventure!)

Gilda:
Aducilo di qua al bastione or ite.

Gilda: *(to Giovanna)*
Let him leave by the terrace door.

Duca:
Di' m'amerai tu?

Duke:
Tell me, do you love me?

Gilda:
E voi?

Gilda:
And you?

Duca:
L'intera vita, poi.

Duke:
Eternally.

Duca e Gilda:
Non più, non più, partite.

Duke and Gilda:
No more, leave.

Vivacissimo
DUKE

Addio, addio, speranza ed anima sol tu sarai per me.	Farewell, farewell, you alone are my hope and soul.
Addio, addio, vivrà immutabile l'affetto mio per te.	Farewell, farewell, our love will be constant. I will live only for you.

Giovanna escorts the Duke into the house.
Gilda remains, gazing at him blissfully as he leaves.

Gilda: **Gilda:**
Gualtier Maldè! Nome di lui sì amato,   Walter Maldè! The name of my lover is
scolpisciti nel core innamorato!   carved in my enchanted heart!

Allegro moderato

Caro nome che il mio cor festi primo palpitar, le delizie dell'amor mi dêi sempre rammentar!	Dearest name, the first love to throb in my heart, I will always remember the delights of love that you have brought to me!
Col pensiero il mio desir a te sempre ognora volerà, e pur l'ultimo sospir, caro nome, tuo sarà!	My thoughts and desires will always be with you, and if it is my last sigh, dear name, it will always be yours!

Gilda enters the house, and then reappears on the terrace,
rapturously watching her lover disappear into the night.

Borsa: **Borsa:** *(pointing to Gilda)*
È là.   There she is.

Ceprano: **Ceprano:**
Miratela.   Look at her.

Cortigiani:.   **Courtiers:**
Oh quanto è bella!   Look how beautiful she is!

Marullo: **Marullo:**
Par fata od angiol.   Like a fairy or an angel.

Cortigiani:
L'amante è quella di Rigoletto!

Courtiers:
That woman is Rigoletto's lover!

Rigoletto appears.

Rigoletto:
(Riedo! Perché?)

Rigoletto: *(upon seeing the courtiers)*
(What can this mean?)

Borsa:
Silenzio, all'opra, badate a me.

Borsa: *(to the courtiers)*
Quiet, there's work to do, listen to me.

Rigoletto:
(Ah da quel vecchio fui maledetto!)

Rigoletto:
(It was that curse from that old man!)

Rigoletto runs into Borsa.

Chi è là?

Who's there?

Borsa:
Tacete, c'è Rigoletto.

Borsa: *(to the courtiers)*
Quiet, there's Rigoletto.

Ceprano:
Vittoria doppia! L'uccideremo.

Ceprano:
A double triumph! Let's kill him.

Borsa:
No, ché domani più rideremo.

Borsa:
No, because we want to laugh tomorrow.

Marullo:
Or tutto aggiusto.

Marullo:
Let's make peace with him.

Rigoletto:
Chi parla qua?

Rigoletto:
Who's talking over there?

Marullo:
Ehi Rigoletto? Di'!

Marullo:
Hey Rigoletto? Speak!

Rigoletto:
Chi va là?

Rigoletto: *(in an angry voice)*
Who goes there?

Marullo:
Eh non mangiarci! Son...

Marullo:
Don't be so irritable! We are...

Rigoletto:
Chi?

Rigoletto:
Who?

Marullo:
Marullo.

Marullo:
Marullo.

Rigoletto:
In tanto bujo lo sguardo è nullo.

Rigoletto:
It's hard to see in such darkness.

Marullo:
Qui ne condusse ridevol cosa, torre a
Ceprano vogliam la sposa.

Marullo:
We're here to have some fun. We want to
abduct Ceprano's wife.

Rigoletto:
(Ohimè respiro!)
Ma come entrare?

Rigoletto: *(expressing relief)*
(I can breathe again!)
How can you enter the house?

Marullo:
La vostra chiave?

Marullo: *(aside to Ceprano)*
Where's your key?
(aside to Rigoletto)

Non dubitare. Non dee mancarci lo
stratagemma.

Don't worry. Every detail has been
planned.

Marullo gives the key to Rigoletto.

Ecco le chiavi.

Here's the key.

Rigoletto:
Sento il tuo stemma.
(Ah terror vano fu dunque il mio!)
N'è là il palazzo, con voi son 'io.

Rigoletto:
I can feel it's crest.
(It was just me, my unnecessary fears!)
She's there in the palace, I'm with you.

Marullo:
Siam mascherati.

Marullo:
We are masked.

Rigoletto:
Ch'io pur mi mascheri a me una larva?

Rigoletto:
It's so dark, do I need a mask too?

Marullo:
Sì, pronta è già.Terrai la scala.

Marullo:
Yes, we're ready. Hold the ladder.

Marullo masks Rigoletto, and binds a handkerchief over his eyes.
Rigoletto, unaware of where he is, holds the ladder beneath the terrace of his own house.

Rigoletto:
Fitta è la tenebra.

Rigoletto:
It's so dark.

Marullo:
La benda cieco e sordo il fa.

Marullo: *(to the courtiers)*
With the mask, he's both deaf and blind.

Some courtiers ascend the terrace and break open the door.
They descend to the lower floor and open the door for the other courtiers.

Tutti:
Zitti, zitti moviamo a vendetta,
ne sia colto or che meno l'aspetta.
Derisore sì audace costante a sua volta
schernito sarà!
Cheti, cheti, rubiamgli l'amante,
e la corte doman riderà.

All:
Quietly, we achieve our vengeance,
without a word or even a sound.
We will scorn the man for his incessant,
audacious mockery!
Swiftly, cautiously, we'll abduct his lover,
and tomorrow the court will ridicule him.

Some courtiers exit the house carrying Gilda, who has been blindfolded with a
handkerchief. As they escape with her, she drops her scarf.

Gilda:
Soccorso, padre mio!

Gilda: *(from the distance)*
Father, help me!

Cortigiani:
Vittoria!

Courtiers:
Victory!

Gilda:
Aita!

Gilda: *(from further away)*
Help me!

Rigoletto:
Non han finito ancor!
Qual derisione!

Rigoletto:
They haven't finished yet!
What jesting!

Rigoletto places his hands to his eyes.

Sono bendato!

My eyes are bandaged!

Rigoletto tears off the bandage and mask.
He picks up a lantern left by one of the courtiers,
and recognizes Gilda's scarf on the ground.
He rushes into the house and returns dragging Giovanna.
He stares at her in bewilderment, tries to express his agony, but he cannot.
He realizes that Gilda has been abducted; in anguish,
he attributes the horrible event to Monterone's curse.

Ah!Ah! Ah! La maledizione!

Ah! Ah!Ah! The curse!

Act II

An hall in the Duke's palace. The doors to the Duke's bedroom are closed.
On each side of the doors there is a portrait respectively of the Duke and the Duchess.
The Duke enters the in great agitation.

Duca:
Ella mi fu rapita!
E quando, o ciel?
Ne'brevi istanti, prima che il mio presagio
interno sull'orma corsa ancora mi
spingesse!

Schiuso era l'uscio!
E la magion deserta!
E dove ora sarà quell'angiol caro?
Colei che prima potè in questo core destar
la fiamma di costanti affetti?

Colei sì pura, al cui modesto sguardo
quasi spinto a virtù talor mi credo!
Ella mi fu rapita!
E chi l'ardiva?
Ma ne avrò vendetta, lo chiede il pianto
della mia diletta.

Duke:
She has overwhelmed me!
Heaven, when did this happen to me?
All of a sudden, I could not rest, and in
my anxiety, I was compelled to return to
her!

The doors of the house were open!
And the house was deserted!
And where was my dear angel?
Why has she seduced my heart and
awakened flames of love?

She is indeed pure and virtuous, and has
such a charming glance!
She has overwhelmed me!
And who would dare to abduct her?
But I will have revenge, and seek to dry
the tears of my beloved.

Adagio
DUKE

Par - mi   veder le la - grime   scorren - ti da quel cig-lio,

Parmi veder le lagrime scorrenti da quel
ciglio, quando fra il dubbio e l'ansia del
subito periglio, dell'amor nostro memore,
il suo Gualtier chiamò.

I seem to see tears running from those
eyes, calling in doubt and anxiety from
her sudden danger. Your Walter
remembers our love and calls to you.

Ned ei potea soccorrerti, cara fanciulla
amata, ei che vorria coll'anima farti
quaggiù beata; ei che le sfere agli angeli,
per te non invidiò.

If I could help you, dearest love, and with
all my soul make you blessed here; I
would not envy you in the realm of the
angels.

Marullo, Borsa, Ceprano and courtiers enter the hall in agitation.

Borsa, Marullo, Ceprano:
Duca, duca!

Borsa, Marullo, Ceprano:
Duke, Duke!

Duca:
Ebben?

Duke:
What is the news?

Borsa, Marullo, Ceprano:
L'amante fu rapita a Rigoletto.

Borsa, Marullo, Ceprano:
We have seized Rigoletto's lover!

Duca:
Come? E donde?

Duke:
How? Where is she?

Borsa, Marullo, Ceprano:
Dal suo tetto.

Borsa, Marullo, Ceprano:
From her home.

Duca:
Ah, ah! Dite, come fu?

Duke:
Oh! Tell me, how did it happen?

Borsa, Marullo, Ceprano:
Scorrendo uniti remota via, brev'ora dopo
caduto il dì, come previsto ben s'era in
pria, rara beltà ci si scoprì.

Borsa, Marullo, Ceprano:
It was dusk, and we were all together in a
remote street. Like a vision out of the
shadows, we discovered this rare beauty.

Era l'amante di Rigoletto, che, vista
appena, si dileguò.
Già di rapirla s'avea il progetto,quando il
buffone ver noi spuntò;
che di Ceprano noi la contessa rapir
volessimo, stolto credé;
la scala, quindi, all'uopo messa, bendato,
ei stesso ferma tenè.
Salimmo, e rapidi la giovinetta a noi
riusciva quindi asportar.
Quand'ei s'accorse della vendettarestò
scornato ad imprecar, ad imprecar.

She was Rigoletto's lover. We saw for an
instant, and then she vanished.
We decided to abduct her, but Rigoletto
saw us and interrupted us;
so we told him we wanted to abduct
Countess Ceprano. He believed the lie;
we had him hold the ladder, we bandaged
his eyes, and he obliged us.
We rapidly went upstairs, grabbed her and
immediately left.
When he discovered our revenge, he
condemned and cursed us.

Duca:
(Cielo! È dessa! La mia diletta!)

Ma dove or trovasi la poveretta?

Duke: *(to himself)*
Heavens! It is she! My adored one!
(to the courtiers)
Where can I find the poor girl?

Borsa, Marullo, Ceprano:
Fu da noi stessi addotta or qui.

Borsa, Marullo, Ceprano:
We've brought her here.

Duca:
(Ah, tutto il ciel non mi rapì!)

Duke: *(becoming joyful at the news)*
(Heaven has not deceived me!)

Possente amor mi chiama, volar io deggio
a lei; il serto mio darei per consolar quel
cor.
Ah! Sappia alfin chi l'ama, conosca alfin
chi sono, apprenda ch'anco in trono ha
degli schiavi Amor.

The [power of love calls me. I must
possess you; I would give my crown to
console that heart.
Finally she will know it is that loves her,
she will know who I am, that the crown is
a slave of Love.

Borsa, Marullo, Ceprano:
Oh qual pensier or l'agita, come cangiò
d'umor!

Borsa, Marullo, Ceprano:
Look how his agitation has suddenly
changed to happiness!

The Duke rushes to his bedroom.
Rigoletto is heard from outside.

Marullo:
Povero Rigoletto!

Marullo:
Poor Rigoletto!

Rigoletto:
La rà, la rà, la la, la rà, la rà, la rà, la rà la
rà, la la, la rà, la rà.

Rigoletto:
La ra, la ra, la la, la ra, la ra, la ra, la ra la
ra, la la, la ra, la ra.

Tutti:
Ei vien! Silenzio.

All:
Here he comes! Quiet.

Rigoletto enters the hall, nonchalant and pretending indifference.

Borsa, Marullo, Ceprano:
Oh buon giorno, Rigoletto.

Borsa, Marullo, Ceprano:
Good morning, Rigoletto.

Rigoletto:
(Han tutti fatto il colpo!)

Rigoletto:
(They're all conspirators!)

Ceprano:
Ch'hai di nuovo, buffon?

Ceprano:
What's new, jester?

Rigoletto:
Ch'hai di nuovo, buffon?
Che dell'usato più noioso voi siete.

Rigoletto: *(imitating Ceprano)*
What's new, jester?
You seem unusually annoyed.

Borsa, Marullo, Ceprano:
Ah! Ah! Ah!

Borsa, Marullo, Ceprano: *(laughing)*
Hah! Hah! Hah!

Rigoletto:
La rà, la rà, la la la rà, la rà, la rà, la rà.

(Ove l'avran nascosta?)

Borsa, Marullo, Ceprano:
(Guardate com'è inquieto!)

Rigoletto:
La rà, la rà, la rà, la rà, la rà, la rà, la rà, la rà, la rà, la rà, la rà.

Borsa, Marullo, Ceprano:
Sì! Sì! Guardate com'è inquieto!

Rigoletto:
Son felice che nulla a voi nuocesse l'aria di questa notte.

Marullo:
Questa notte!

Rigoletto:
Sì. Oh fu il bel colpo!

Marullo:
S'ho dormito sempre!

Rigoletto:
Ah, voi dormiste! Avrò dunque sognato!

Rigoletto: *(wandering inquisitively)*
La ra, la ra, la la la ra, la ra, la ra, la ra.

(Where could they have hidden her?)

Borsa, Marullo, Ceprano:
(Look at how agitated he is!)

Rigoletto:
La ra, la ra, la la, la ra, la ra, la ra, la ra la ra, la la, la ra, la ra.

Borsa, Marullo, Ceprano:
Yes! Yes! Look how agitated he is!

Rigoletto: *(to Marullo)*
I'm pleased that none of you were harmed by this evening's air.

Marullo:
This evening!

Rigoletto:
Yes, it was quite a good joke!

Marullo:
I have never slept better!

Rigoletto:
You slept! I wish I could have slept!

Rigoletto finds a handkerchief and seizes it.

La rà, la rà, la la, la rà, la rà, la rà, la la.

Borsa, Marullo, Ceprano:
(Ve', come tutto osserva!)

Rigoletto:
(Non è il suo.)
Dorme il Duca tuttor?

Borsa, Marullo, Ceprano:
Sì, dorme ancora.

La ra, la ra, la la, la ra, la ra, la ra, la la.

Borsa, Marullo, Ceprano:
(Look at how he scrutinizes everything!)

Rigoletto: *(looking at the handkerchief)*
(It's not hers.)
Is the Duke still sleeping?

Borsa, Marullo, Ceprano:
Yes, he's still sleeping.

Paggio:
Al suo sposo parlar vuol la Duchessa.

Page:
The Duchess wishes to speak to her husband.

Ceprano:
Dorme.

Ceprano:
He's sleeping.

Paggio:
Qui or or con voi non era?

Page:
Wasn't he here with you just before?

Borsa:
È a caccia

Borsa:
He's hunting.

Paggio:
Senza paggi! Senz'armi!

Page:
Without pages! Without weapons!

Borsa, Marullo, Ceprano:
E non capisci che per ora vedere non può alcuno?

Borsa, Marullo, Ceprano:
Don't you understand that he doesn't want to see anyone now?

Rigoletto:
Ah! Ella è qui dunque!
Ella è col Duca!

Rigoletto:
She is with him!
She is with the Duke!

Borsa, Marullo, Ceprano:
Chi?

Borsa, Marullo, Ceprano:
Who?

Rigoletto:
La giovin che sta notte al mio tetto rapiste.
Ma la saprò riprender. Ella è là.

Rigoletto:
The young girl you abducted from my house this evening.
I know I can recover her. She is there.

Borsa, Marullo, Ceprano:
Se l'amante perdesti, la ricerca altrove.

Borsa, Marullo, Ceprano:
If you lost your lover, find her elsewhere.

Rigoletto:
Io vo' mia figlia.

Rigoletto:
I want my daughter.

Borsa, Marullo, Ceprano:
La sua figlia!

Borsa, Marullo, Ceprano:
His daughter!

Rigoletto:
Sì, la mia figlia.
D'una tal vittoria che?
Adesso non ridete?
Ella è là! La vogl'io la renderete!

Rigoletto:
Yes, my daughter.
What kind of victory is that?
You're not laughing now?
She is there! I want you to return her!

Andante mosso agitato
RIGOLETTO

Cor-ti -giani,   vil razza   da-nnata,   per qual prezzo vendeste il mio cor?

Cortigiani, vil razza dannata, per qual
prezzo vendeste il mio bene?
A voi nulla per l'oro sconviene!

Courtiers, damned vile race, for what
price have you sold my treasure?
For you, there is no longer decency!

Ma mia figlia è impagabil tesor.
La rendete o, se pur disarmata, questa
man per voi fora cruenta;
nulla in terra più l'uomo paventa, se dei
figli difende l'onor.

But my daughter is a priceless treasure.
Return her, or be defenseless against this
hand that will pierce your skull;
nothing on earth is more frightening than
a father defending his daughter's honor.

Quella porta, assassini, assassini,
m'aprite, la porta, la porta, assassini,
m'aprite.

That door, assassins, assassins,
open it, the door, the door, assassins, open
it.

Ah! Voi tutti a me contro venite!
Tutti contra me!
Ah! Ebben, piango, Marullo, signore, tu
ch'hai l'alma gentil come il core, dimmi
tu dove l'hanno nascosta?
È là? Non è vero?
Tu taci! Ohimè!

Ah! You're all against me!
All against me!
Well, I am crying. Marullo, sir, you have a
gentle soul like your heart, tell me where
you have hidden her?
Is she there? Is that true?
You are quiet! How unfortunate!

Miei signori, perdono, pietate, al
vegliardo la figlia ridate.
Ridonarla a voi nulla ora costa, tutto al
mondo è tal figlia per me.
Pietà, pietà, signori!

My lords, pardon, pity, and return the
daughter of an old man.
Return her, it costs you nothing, my
daughter is everything in the world to me.
Mercy, my lords!

Gilda rushes from the room and throws herself in her father's arms.

Gilda:
Mio padre!

Gilda:
Father!

Rigoletto:
Dio! Mia Gilda! Signori in essa è tutta la
mia famiglia.

Rigoletto:
God! My Gilda! Lords, in this girl you see
my entire family.

Non temer più nulla, angelo mio fu
scherzo! Non è vero?

Don't fear anything, my angel, it was all a
joke! Isn't that true?

Io che pur piansi or rido.
E tu a che piangi?

I was weeping, but now I rejoice.
And why are you crying?

Gilda:
Ah l'onta, padre mio.

Gilda:
Father, I was dishonored.

Rigoletto:
Cielo! Che dici?

Rigoletto:
Heavens! What did you say?

Gilda:
Arrosir voglio innanzi a voi soltanto.

Gilda:
I want to blush, and be alone with you.

Rigoletto:
Ite di qua, voi tutti.
Se il duca vostro d'appressarsi osasse,
ch'ei non entri, gli dite, e ch'io ci sono.

Rigoletto: *(imperiously to the courtiers)*
All of you leave.
If the Duke dares to approach us, tell him
to stay away.

Courtiers:
(Coi fanciulli e co'dementi spesso giova il
simular. Partiam pur, ma quel ch'ei tenti
non lasciamo d'osservar.)

Courtiers:
(We cannot pretend to help insane men
with their children. Let's leave, we don't
want to observe his agony.)

The courtiers exit, leaving Rigoletto and Gilda alone.

Rigoletto:
Parla, siam soli.

Rigoletto:
Speak to me, we're alone.

Gilda:
(Ciel! Dammi coraggio!)

Gilda:
(Heaven! Give me courage!)

Andantino
GILDA

Tutte le fe - ste al tem - pio   *mentre prega - va Id - dio,*

Tutte le feste al tempio mentre pregava
Iddio, bello e fatale un giovine offriasi al
guardo mio, se i labbri nostri tacquero,
dagl'occhi il cor, il cor parlò.

At the festivals at church, while I was
praying to God, a handsome and
irresistible man offered to protect me, our
lips could not utter what was in our
hearts.

Furtivo fra le tenebre sol ieri a me
giungeva. Sono studente, povero,
commosso mi diceva, e con ardente
palpito amor mi protestò.

Partì, il mio core aprivasi a speme più
gradita, quando improvvisi apparvero
color che m'han rapita, e a forza qui
m'addussero nell'ansia più crudel.

Rigoletto:
Ah! (Solo per me l'infamia a te chiedeva,
o Dio, ch'ella potesse ascendere quanto
caduto er'io.
Ah! Presso del patibolo bisogna ben
l'altare!
Ma tutto ora scompare, l'altare, si
rovesciò!)

Piangi! Piangi fanciulla, fanciulla piangi,
scorrer, scorrer fa il pianto sul mio cor.

Gilda:
Padre, in voi parla un angel per me
consolator.

Rigoletto:
Compiuto pur quanto a fare mi resta,
lasciare potremo quest'aura funesta.

Gilda:
Sì.

Rigoletto:
(E tutto un sol giorno cangiare potè!)

Yesterday, as evening fell, he stood before
me. He told me he was a poor student,
and ardently declared his love for me.

After he left, my heart became stirred by
profound hope. Then in the darkness they
abducted me, and brought me by force to
experience this cruel anguish.

Rigoletto: *(to himself)*
Ah! (I prayed to God that I might avoid
this disgrace, that she would be able to
avoid the evil that has fallen on me.
Ah! An altar is needed next to the
executioner's scaffold!
But all has disappeared, the altar, it has
been turned back!)

(to Gilda)
Cry! Cry child, child cry,
your tears are flowing in my heart.

Gilda:
Father, a consoling angel speaks from
your voice.

Rigoletto:
What remains for us is to leave this
sinister place.

Gilda:
Yes.

Rigoletto: *(to himself)*
(And all in one day our fate has changed!)

Monterone, escorted by armed guards, passes through the hall.

Usciere:
Schiudete, ire al carcere Monteron dee.

Ushers:
Open up, so Monterone can go to his cell.

Monterone stops before the portrait of the Duke.

Monterone:
Poichè fosti invano da me maledetto, nè
un fulmine o un ferro colpiva il tuo petto,
felice pur anco, o duca, vivrai!

Monterone:
So my curse has been in vain, neither a
thunderbolt or steel has entered your
breast. Duke, you are still live happily!

Monterone is led away by the guards.

Rigoletto:
No, vecchio t'inganni,
un vindice avrai!

Rigoletto:
No, old man, you are mistaken, you will
yet have vengeance!

Rigoletto:

Rigoletto: *(addressing the Duke's portrait)*

Allegro vivo
RIGOLETTO

Sì,   ven - det - ta, tre-men - da ven - det - ta,

Sì, vendetta, tremenda vendetta di
quest'anima è solo desio, di punirti già
l'ora s'affretta, che fatale per te tuonerà.
Come fulmin scagliato da Dio, te colpire
il buffone saprà.

Yes, a frightful vengeance is all that this
soul desires, the fatal thunder of your
punishment will arrive quickly.
Like a thunderbolt from God, you will
know that the blow came from the jester.

Gilda:
O mio padre, qual gioia feroce balenarvi
ne gl'occhi vegg'io!
Perdonate, a noi pure una voce di
perdono dal cielo verrà.
(Mi tradiva, pur l'amo, gran Dio!
Per l'ingrato ti chiedo pietà!)

Gilda:
My father, what ferocious joy flashes
from you old eyes!
Pardon him. Let a pure voice from
Heaven grant him forgiveness!
(He betrayed me, but I love him!
Oh God, I beg forgiveness for the wicked
man!)

Rigoletto and Gilda exit.

ACT III

The shore of the Mincio River. There is a two-story house: a rustic Inn.

It is night. Gilda and Rigoletto are outside the house; inside, Sparafucile is seated at a table, polishing his belt, and unaware that Rigoletto and Gilda are outside.

Rigoletto:
E l'ami?

Rigoletto:
Do you still love him?

Gilda:
Sempre.

Gilda:
Always.

Rigoletto:
Pure tempo a guarirne t'ho lasciato.

Rigoletto:
I have left you enough time to cure yourself of this infatuation.

Gilda:
Io l'amo.

Gilda:
I love him.

Rigoletto:
Povero cor di donna! Ah il vile infame!
Ma ne avrai vendetta, o Gilda!

Rigoletto:
A poor woman's heart! That vile traitor!
But Gilda you will yet have revenge!

Gilda:
Pietà, mio padre!

Gilda:
Father, have mercy!

Rigoletto:
E se tu certa fossi ch'ei ti tradisse,
l'ameresti ancora?

Rigoletto:
If I could convince you that he betrayed you, would you still love him?

Gilda:
Nol so, ma pur m'adora.

Gilda:
I don't know, but he indeed adores me.

Rigoletto:
Egli?

Rigoletto:
He does?

Gilda:
Sì.

Gilda:
Yes.

Rigoletto leads Gilda to the house where they can spy inside.

Rigoletto:
Ebben, osserva dunque.

Rigoletto:
Well, then observe inside.

Gilda:
Un uomo vedo.

Gilda:
I see a man.

Rigoletto:
Per poco attendi.

Rigoletto:
Watch him attentively.

The Duke, disguised as a cavalry officer, is seen inside the Inn.

Gilda:
Ah padre mio!

Gilda: *(startled)*
Oh, father!

Duca:
Due cose, e tosto.

Duke: *(to Sparafucile)*
Two things, right away.

Sparafucile:
Quali?

Sparafucile:
What are they?

Duca:
Una stanza e del vino.

Duke:
A room and wine.

Rigoletto:
(Son questi i suoi costumi!)

Rigoletto:
(Those are his usual adventures!)

Sparafucile:
(Oh il bel zerbino!)

Sparafucile:
(Oh what a dandy!)

Allegretto
DUKE

La donna è mobile qual piuma al vento, muta d'ac-cen - to e di pen-si -e- ro,

Duca:
La donna è mobile qual piuma al vento,
muta d'accento e di pensiero.

Duke:
All women are capricious, like a plume in
the wind, changing their thoughts.

Sempre un amabile leggiadro viso, in
pianto o in riso, è menzognero.

Their face is always amiable, but in tears
or in laughter, they are always deceptive.

È sempre misero chi a lei s'affida, chi le
confida mal cauto il core!

Pur mai non sentesi felice appieno chi su
quel seno non liba amore!

Misfortune always awaits one who trusts
them; one who confides in them must be
cautious in his heart!
But one can never achieve full happiness
if he never tastes love!

Sparafucile places a flask of wine with two glasses on a table.
He then knocks on the ceiling twice with the hilt of his sword.
A smiling young gypsy woman descends the stairs.
The Duke rushes to embrace her, but she is coquettish and teases him.
Meanwhile, Sparafucile exits the Inn to speak with Rigoletto.

Sparafucile:
È là il vostr'uomo.
Viver dee o morire?

Sparafucile:
Your man is in there.
Shall he live or die?

Rigoletto:
Più tardi tornerò l'opra a compire.

Rigoletto:
I'll return later when the deed is
accomplished.

Sparafucile goes off behind the house toward the river.
Gilda and Rigoletto remain outside the house.
They peer inside and overhear the Duke and Maddalena conversing.

Duca:
Un dì, si ben rammentomi, o bella,
t'incontrai.
Mi piacque di te chiedere, e intesi che qui
stai.
Or sappi, che d'allora sol te quest'alma
adora.

Duke:
One day, if I remember well, beautiful
lady, I met you.
I asked to know your name, and you
intended to remain with me.
Your should know that from then on it is
only you who I adore.

Gilda:
Iniquo!

Gilda:
Traitor!

Maddalena:
Ah, ah! E vent'altre appresso le scorda
forse adesso?
Ha un'aria il signorino da vero libertino.

Maddalena:
Hah, hah! And later you seem to forget
them all?
You have an air of a lord, a true libertine.

Duca:
Sì! Un mostro son.

Duke: *(trying to embrace her)*
Yes! I am a monster.

Gilda:
Ah padre mio!

Gilda: *(observing them)*
Oh father!

Maddalena:
Lasciatemi, stordito.

Duca:
Ah, che fracasso!

Maddalena:
Stia saggio.

Duca:
E tu sii docile,
non farmi tanto chiasso.
Ogni saggezza chiudesi nel gaudio e
nell'amore.

The Duke takes Maddalena's hand.

La bella mano candida!.

Maddalena:
Scherzate voi, signore.

Duca:
No, no.

Maddalena:
Son brutta.

Duca:
Abbracciami.

Gilda:
Iniquo!

Maddalena:
Ebro!

Duca:
D'amor ardente.

Maddalena:
Signor l'indifferente, vi piace canzonar?

Duca:
No, no, ti vo'sposar.

Maddalena:
Ne voglio la parola.

Maddalena:
Leave me, you inconsiderate man.

Duke:
Oh, what bickering!

Maddalena:
This is nonsense.

Duke:
And you are so gentle,
don't excite me so much.
Every wise indulges in the pleasures of
love.

Such a beautiful white hand!

Maddalena:
You're playing games with me, sir.

Duke:
Not at all.

Maddalena:
I am ugly.

Duke:
Embrace me.

Gilda:
Betrayer!

Maddalena:
You're drunk!

Duke: *(laughing)*
From ardent love.

Maddalena:
Do you want me to sing?

Duke:
No, no, I want to marry you.

Maddalena:
I don't want to hear that word.

Duca:
Amabile figliuola!

Duke: *(ironically)*
Such a gracious young woman!

Rigoletto:
E non ti basta ancor?

Rigoletto: *(to Gilda)*
Is that enough for you?

Gilda:
Iniquo traditor!

Gilda:
Wicked traitor!

Andante
DUKE

Bel- la figlia del-l'a - mo - re, schiavo son de'vezzi tuo - i,

Duca:
Bella figlia dell'amore, schiavo son
de'vezzi tuoi;
con un detto sol tu puoi le mie pene
consolar.
Vieni e senti del mio core il frequente
palpitar. Con un detto sol tu puoi le mie
pene consolar.

Duke:
Beautiful daughter of love, I am a slave to
you charms;
with one word you can console my
suffering.
Come and feel my heart pounding. With
one word, you can console my suffering.

Maddalena:
Ah! Ah! Rido ben di core, chè tai baie
costan poco, quanto valga il vostro gioco,
mel credete so apprezzar.
Sono avvezza, bel signore ad un simile
scherzar.

Maddalena:
Hah! Hah! My heart laughs, your jesting
is so casual, and your game so trivial. I
know well how to appreciate honey. I'm
accustomed to a handsome man and such
games.

Gilda:
Ah così parlar d'amore a me pur l'infame
ho udito!
Infelice cor tradito, per angoscia non
scoppiar.

Gilda:
The way he talks of love, I have truly
witnessed his betrayal!
Oh my unhappy betrayed heart. I don't
want to die of anguish.

Rigoletto:
Taci, il piangere non vale; ch'ei mentiva
or sei sicura.
Taci, e mia sarà la cura la vendetta
d'affrettar.
Sì, pronta fia sarà fatale, io saprollo
fulminar.

Rigoletto: *(to Gilda)*
Quiet, it's not worth tears; you can be
certain he is has lied to you.
Quiet, my cure will be a quick vengeance.
Yes, soon it will be fatal, and I will wield
it like a lightning bolt.

M'odi! Ritorna a casa oro prendi, un
destriero, una veste viril che t'apprestai,
e per Verona parti.
Sarovvi io pur doman.

Listen to me! Go home, take money, a
steed, a man's clothes to disguise
yourself, and go to Verona.
I'll meet you there tomorrow.

Gilda:
Or venite.

Gilda:
Come with me now.

Rigoletto:
Impossibil.

Rigoletto:
Impossible.

Gilda:
Tremo.

Gilda:
I'm afraid.

Rigoletto:
Va!

Rigoletto:
Go!

*Gilda departs. The Duke and Maddalena remain in conversation inside the Inn.
Rigoletto goes behind the Inn and returns with Sparafucile,
and then counts out money for him.*

Venti scudi hai tu detto?
Eccone dieci; e dopo l'opra il resto.
Ei qui rimane?

Did you say twenty scudos?
Here are ten; and after the deed the rest.
Will you be here?

Sparafucile:
Sì.

Sparafucile:
Yes.

Rigoletto:
Alla mezzanotte ritornerò.

Rigoletto:
I'll return at midnight.

Sparafucile:
Non cale. A gettarlo nel fiume basto io
solo.

Sparafucile:
It's not necessary. I can throw him in the
river myself.

Rigoletto:
No, no, il vo' far io stesso.

Rigoletto:
No, no, I want to do it myself.

Sparafucile:
Sia! Il suo nome?

Sparafucile:
All right! What's his name?

Rigoletto:
Vuoi saper anche il mio?
Egli è Delitto, Punizion son io.

Rigoletto:
Do you want to know mine too?
He is Crime, I am Punishment.

As Rigoletto departs, lightning flashes.

Sparafucile:
La tempesta è vicina!
Più scura fia la notte.

Sparafucile:
The storm is near!
The night is getting darker.

Duca:
Maddalena!

Duke: *(seizing Maddalena)*
Maddalena!

Maddalena:
Aspettate, mio fratello viene.

Maddalena: *(resisting him)*
Wait, my brother is coming.

Duca:
Che importa?

Duke:
Why should that matter?

Maddalena:
Tuona!

Maddalena:
There is thunder!

Sparafucile enters the Inn.

Sparafucile:
E pioverà fra poco.

Sparafucile:
It will be raining soon.

Duca:
Tanto meglio! Tu dormerai in scuderia,
all'inferno, ove vorrai.

Duke:
All the better! You sleep in the stable, or
with the devil, whatever you wish.

Sparafucile:
Oh grazie!

Sparafucile:
How gracious!

Maddalena:
(Ah, no, partite.)

Maddalena: *(aside to the Duke)*
(Oh, no, you must leave.)

Duca:
(Con tal tempo?)

Duke:
(You refuse me?)

Sparafucile:
Son venti scudi d'oro.

Ben felice d'offrirvi la mia stanza, se a
voi piace tosto a vederla andiamo.

Sparafucile: *(aside to Maddalena)*
There are twenty scudos in gold.
(to the Duke)
It will be my pleasure to offer you my
room, if you want to see it, let's go.

Sparafucile takes a light and goes toward the ladder leading to the second floor.

Duca:
Ebben!
Sono con te, presto, vediamo.

Duke:
Very well!
I'll go you, quickly, let's see.

The Duke whispers something to Maddalena and then follows Sparafucile.

Maddalena:
Povero giovin! Grazioso tanto!
Dio, qual notte è questa!

Maddalena:
That poor young man! So gracious!
God, what a dreadful night this is!

Duca:
Si dorme all'aria aperta?
Bene, Bene! Buona notte.

Duke: *(from upstairs)*
Sleeping in the open?
Good, good! Good evening.

Sparafucile:
Signor, vi guardi Iddio!

Sparafucile:
Sir, may God watch over you!

The Duke removes his hat and sword.

Duca:
Breve sonno dormiam, stanco son io.

La donna è mobile qual piuma al vento,
muta d'accento e di pensiero.

Duke:
A short sleep, I'm quite tired.

All women are capricious, like a plume in
the wind, changing their thoughts.

The Duke falls asleep. Meanwhile, Maddalena sits at a table with Sparafucile.
Sparafucile drinks from the bottle left by the Duke.
Both become preoccupied with serious thoughts, and then,
Maddalena breaks the silence.

Maddalena::
È amabile in vero cotal giovinotto!

Maddalena:
That young man is genuinely amiable!

Sparafucile:
Oh sì, venti scudi ne dà di prodotto.

Sparafucile:
Oh, yes, he's produced twenty scudos for
us.

Maddalena:
Sol venti? Son pochi!
Valeva di più.

Maddalena:
Only twenty? That's nothing!
He's worth more.

Sparafucile:
La spada, s'ei dorme, va portami giù.

Sparafucile:
My sword is idle, go get it for me.

Maddalena ascends the stairs and gazes at the Duke.

Maddalena:
Peccato è pur bello!

Maddalena:
It's a shame, he's so handsome!

Gilda appears outside the Inn. She is dressed in male clothes, with boots and spurs.
She slowly approaches the Inn and observes Sparafucile.

Gilda:
Ah, più non ragiono!
Amor mi trascina!
Mio padre, perdono.
Qual notte d'orrore!
Gran Dio, che accadrà!

Gilda:
I can't bear it!
My lover has betrayed me!
Father, forgive me!
What a horrible night!
Oh, God, what a fate!

Maddalena returns to the ground floor and lays the Duke's sword on the table.

Maddalena:
Fratello?

Maddalena:
Brother?

Gilda:
Chi parla?

Gilda: *(spying on them)*
Who is that speaking?

Sparafucile:
Al diavol ten va

Sparafucile:
The devil awaits.

Maddalena:
Somiglia un Apollo quel giovine,
io l'amo, ei m'ama, riposi, nè più
l'uccidiamo.

Maddalena:
That young man looks like an Apollo.
I love him, and he loves me. Reconsider
and let's not kill him.

Gilda:
Oh cielo!

Gilda:
Oh Heavens!

Sparafucile:
Rattoppa quel sacco.

Sparafucile: *(throwing her a sack)*
Mend this sack.

Maddalena:
Perchè?

Maddalena:
Why?

Sparafucile:
Entr'esso il tuo Apollo, sgozzato da me,
gettar dovrò al fiume.

Sparafucile:
For your Apollo to be thrown in the river,
after I slaughter him.

Gilda:
L'inferno qui vedo!

Gilda:
I am witnessing hell!

Maddalena:
Eppure il danaro salvarti scommetto,
serbandolo in vita.

Sparafucile:
Difficile il credo.

Maddalena:
M'ascolta, anzi facil ti svelo un progetto.
De'scudi già dieci dal gobbo ne avesti;
venire cogl'altri più tardi il vedrai.
Uccidilo e, venti allora ne avrai.
Così tutto il prezzo goder si potrà.

Gilda:
Che sento! Mio padre!

Sparafucile:
Uccider quel gobbo!
Che diavol dicesti!
Un ladro son forse?
Son forse un bandito?
Qual altro cliente da me fu tradito?
Mi paga quest'uomo, fedele m'avrà.

Maddalena:
Ah, grazia per esso.

Sparafucile:
È duopo ch'ei muoia.

Maddalena:
Fuggire il fo adesso!

Gilda:
Oh buona figliuola!

Sparafucile:
Gli scudi perdiamo.

Maddalena:
È ver!

Sparafucile:
Lascia fare.

Maddalena:
If it was not for the money, I bet I could
persuade you to spare his life.

Sparafucile:
Don't even consider it.

Maddalena:
Listen to me. I have a better plan to you.
The hunchback already gave you ten
scudos, and he's coming later with the
rest. Kill him and then you'll have twenty.
It will be the full price and I'll be thrilled.

Gilda:
What do I hear! My father!

Sparafucile:
Kill the hunchback!
What devil speaks to me!
Am I a thief?
Am I a bandit?
Did I ever betray a client?
The man paid me and I must be honorable.

Maddalena:
Spare the young man.

Sparafucile:
I'll be killing him later.

Maddalena: *(rushing up the stairs)*
I'll let him escape from you!

Sparafucile:
Such a good woman!

Sparafucile:
We'll lose the money.

Maddalena:
That's true!

Sparafucile:
Let everything be.

Maddalena:
Salvarlo dobbiamo.

Maddalena:
We must save him.

Sparafucile:,
Se pria ch'abbia il mezzo la notte toccato
alcuno qui giunga, per esso morrà.

Sparafucile:
Then instead, whoever arrives here at
midnight will become the victim.

Maddalena:
È buoia la notte, il ciel troppo irato,
nessuno, a quest'ora da qui passerà.

Maddalena:
It's a dark night, and the Heaven's are
angry, no one will come here at this hour.

Gilda:
Oh qual tentazione!
Morir per l'ingrato!
Morire, mio padre! Oh cielo! Pietà!

Gilda:
What a temptation!
To die for that ingrate!
To die, father! Heaven! Mercy!

The violent thunder and lightning ceases. A clock strikes the half-hour.

Sparafucile:
Ancor c'è mezz'ora.

Sparafucile:
There's still a half-hour remaining.

Maddalena:
Attendi, fratello.

Maddalena: *(in tears)*
Wait, brother.

Gilda:
Che! Piange tal donna!
N'è a lui darò aita!
Ah, s'egli al mio amore divenne rubello,
io vo'per la sua gettar la mia vita.

Gilda:
What! A woman is in tears!
Can I let him perish?
Although he has betrayed our love,
I want to die for him.

Gilda knocks at the door.

Maddalena:
Si picchia?

Maddalena:
Who's knocking?

Sparafucile:
Fu il vento.

Sparafucile;
It was the wind.

Gilda knocks again.

Maddalena:
Si picchia, ti dico.

Maddalena:
I'm telling you someone is knocking.

Sparafucile:
È strano! Chi è?

Sparafucile:
That's strange! Who is it?

Gilda:
Pietà d'un mendico; asil per la notte a lui concedete.

Gilda:
Mercy for a friar; please give him shelter for the night.

Maddalena:
Fia lunga tal notte!

Maddalena:
A stranger on such a night!

Sparafucile:
Alquanto attendete.

Sparafucile: *(searching the cupboard)*
I'll find something to give him.

Maddalena:
Su, spicciati, presto, fa l'opra compita; anelo una vita con altra salvar.

Maddalena:
Get moving, quickly complete the job; take a life so another can be saved.

Sparafucile:
Ebbene, son pronto, quell'uscio dischiudi; più ch'altro gli scudi mi preme salvar.

Sparafucile:
Well, I'm ready, open the door; it is more than money that's making me save your prize.

Gilda:
Ah! Presso alla morte, sì giovine, sono! Oh ciel, per gl'empi ti chieggo perdono! Perdona tu, o padre, questa infelice! Sia l'uomo felice ch'or vado a salvar.

Gilda:
I am about to die, my love! Heaven, I ask your forgiveness! Father, forgive this unhappy woman! I save him to make him happy.

Amid thunder and lightning, Gilda knocks on the door again.
Sparafucile places himself behind the door, his dagger raised.

Sparafucile:
Apri.

Sparafucile: *(to Maddalena)*
Open it.

Maddalena:
Entri.

Maddalena:
Come in.

Gilda:
Dio! Loro perdonate!

Gilda:
God! Forgive me!

Gilda enters. Sparafucile closes the door behind her, and then stabs her.
The thunder ceases, but the rain and lightning continue.

In the darkness, there is silence. As the violent storm gradually abates,
Rigoletto, wrapped in his cloak, appears before the Inn.

Rigoletto:
Della vendetta alfin giunge l'istante!
Da trenta dì l'aspetto di vivo sangue a
lagrime piangendo, sotto la larva del
buffon.

Quest'uscio è chiuso!
Ah, non è tempo ancor!
S'attenda. Qual notte di mistero!
Una tempesta in cielo!
In terra un omicidio!
Oh come in vero qui grande mi sento!

Rigoletto:
The moment of vengeance finally arrives!
It has been thirty days of blood and
anguished tears beneath the jester's mask.

The door is closed!
There's not much time left!
I'll wait. What an ominous night!
A storm in the skies!
On earth a murder!
But truthfully, I feel wonderful!

The clock strikes midnight.

Mezza notte!

Midnight!

Rigoletto knocks on the door.

Sparafucile:
Chi è là?

Sparafucile:
Who is it?

Rigoletto:
Son io.

Rigoletto:
It is me.

Sparafucile brings the sack to Rigoletto.

Sparafucile:
Sostate.
È qua spento il vostr'uomo!

Sparafucile:
Wait.
Here is your dead man!

Rigoletto:
Oh gioia! Un lume!

Rigoletto:
What joy! A lamp!

Sparafucile:
Un lume? No, il danaro.
Lesti, all'onda il gettiam.

Sparafucile:
A lamp? No, the money.
Quickly, we'll throw him in the river.

Rigoletto:
No, basto io solo.

Rigoletto: *(gives him a purse)*
No, I will do that.

Sparafucile:
E come vi piace. Qui men atto è il sito più
avanti è più profondo il gorgo. Presto, che
alcun non vi sorprenda.
Buona notte.

Sparafucile:
At your pleasure. Here it is shallow, but
further down the river it is deeper.
Quickly, so no one surprises you.
Good evening.

Sparafucile reenters the Inn.

Rigoletto:
Egli è là! Morto! Oh sì! Vorrei vederlo!
Ma che importa! È ben desso!
Ecco i suoi sproni!
Ora mi guarda, o mondo!
Quest'è un buffone, ed un potente è questo!
Ei sta sotto i miei piedi!
È desso! Oh gioia!
È giunta alfine la tua vendetta, o duolo!

Sia l'onda a lui sepolcro, un sacco il suo lenzuolo! All'onda! All'onda!

Rigoletto:
He is dead! Yes! I want to see him!
But it's not important! It's surely him!
I feel his spurs!
Now world look at me!
This is a jester, and indeed a man of power!
And he remains under my foot!
It is true! What joy!
My greed has vanished, my vengeance finally has arrived!

The waves will be his grave, the sack his shroud! To the waves! To the waves!

As Rigoletto drags the sack toward the river,
he is shocked when he hears the voice of the Duke in the distance.

Duca:
La donna è mobile qual piuma al vento,
muta d'accento e di pensiero.
Sempre un amabile leggiadro viso, in pianto o in riso, è menzognero.

La donna è mobile qual piuma al vento,
muta d'accento e di pensiero.

Duke:
All women are capricious, like a plume in the wind, changing their thoughts.
Their face is always amiable, but deceptive in their tears or laughter.

All women are capricious, like a plume in the wind, changing tone and thought.

Rigoletto:
Qual voce! Illusion notturna è questa!
No, no! Egli è desso!
Maledizione!

Rigoletto:
That voice! It's an illusion of the night!
No, no! He's in here!
Curses!

Rigoletto rushes toward the Inn and knocks on the door.

Olà, dimon bandito!
Chi è mai, chi è qui in sua vece?

Hello, demonic bandit!
Who is it, who is in the sack?

Io tremo, è umano corpo!

I'm trembling, it's a human body!

Rigoletto cuts open the sack. There is a flash of lightning revealing Gilda.

Mia figlia! Dio! Mia figlia!
Ah, no! È impossibil!
Per Verona è in via!
Fu vision! È dessa!

My daughter! My daughter!
No! It's impossible!
She's en route to Verona!
It was a vision! But it is her!

Oh mia Gilda! Fanciulla a me rispondi!
L'assassino mi svela.

My Gilda! Girl answer me!
Tell me who the assassin was.

Rigoletto knocks desperately at the door of the Inn.

Olà? Nessuno! Nessun! Mia figlia? Mia Gilda? Oh mia figlia?	Hello? No one! No one! My daughter? My daughter? Oh, my daughter?

Gilda:
Chi mi chiama?

Gilda:
Who calls me?

Rigoletto:
Ella parla! Si move!
È viva! Oh Dio!
Ah, mio ben solo in terra mi guarda, mi
conosci.

Rigoletto:
She speaks! She moves!
She is alive! Oh God!
Look at me, my only treasure, recognize
me.

Gilda:
Ah, padre mio!

Gilda:
Oh, my father!

Rigoletto:
Qual mistero! Che fu!
Sei tu ferita? Dimmi.

Rigoletto:
What a mystery! By whom!
Are you wounded? Tell me.

Gilda:
L'acciar qui, qui mi piagò.

Gilda: *(indicating her heart)*
The wound, here is where it struck.

Rigoletto:
Chi t'ha colpita?

Rigoletto:
Who struck you?

Andante
GILDA

V'ho ingannato   colpevole fu - i   l'amai   troppo   ora muoio per lu - i!

Gilda:
V'ho l'ingannato, colpevole fui, l'amai
troppo, ora muoio per lui!

Gilda:
I have deceived you. I was guilty. I loved
him too much. Now I die for him!

Rigoletto:
(Dio tremendo! Ella stessa fu côlta dallo
stral di mia giusta vendetta!)

Rigoletto:
(Frightful God! She herself was struck by
the darts of my righteous vengeance!)

Angiol caro, mi guarda, m'ascolta,
parla, parlami, figlia diletta!

Dear angel, look at me, listen to me,
speak, speak to me, precious daughter!

Gilda:
Ah, ch'io taccia! A me, a lui perdonate!
Benedite, alla figlia, o mio padre.

Gilda:
I accuse myself! Forgive him for me!
Oh father, bless your daughter.

Andante
GILDA

Lassù in cielo, vi - ci-no al -la madre,   in e - terno per voi preghiero,

Lassù in cielo, vicina alla madre, in eterno
per voi pregherò.

Up there, in Heaven, near my mother,
I will forever pray for you.

Rigoletto:
Non morir mio tesoro, pietade mia
colomba lasciarmi non dêi.

Rigoletto:
Don't die my treasure, have pity my dove,
don't leave me.

Se t'involi qui sol rimarrei non morire,
o qui teco morrò!

If you leave me here alone I will mourn,
don't die, or I will also die!

Gilda:
Non più. A lui perdonate mio padre, ad...
dio!

Gilda:
I can't anymore. Forgive him father,
fare..well!

Gilda dies.

Rigoletto:
Gilda! Mia Gilda! È morta!
Ah! La maledizione!!

Rigoletto:
Gilda! My Gilda! She is dead!
Ah! The curse!

Rigoletto tears at his hair, and then faints as he falls on Gilda's corpse.

RIGOLETTO

Discography

1916   Baldini (Rigoletto); Zerni (Gilda); Broccardi (Duke); Pezzati (Maddalena);
            Bettoni (Sparafucile);
            Sabajno (Conductor)

1927   Piazza (Rigoletto); Pagliughi (Gilda); Folgar (Duke); de Christoff (Maddalena);
            Baccaloni (Sparafucile);
            La Scala Chorus and Orchestra;
            Sabajno (Conductor)

1930   Stracciari (Rigoletto); Capsir (Gilda); Borgioli (Duke); Bassi (Maddalena);
            Dominici (Sparafucile);
            La Scala Chorus and Orchestra;
            Molajoli (Conductor)

1950   Warren (Rigoletto); Berger (Gilda); Peerce (Duke); Merriman (Maddalena);
            Tajo (Sparafucile;
            Shaw Chorale/RCA Orchestra;
            Cellini (Conductor)

1951   Petrov (Rigoletto); Orlandini (Gilda); Sarri (Duke); Melani (Maddalenna);
            Frosini (Sparafucile);
            Florence Festival Chorus and Orchestra;
            Ghiglia (Conductor)

1952   (Live performance: Mexico City)
            Campolonghi (Rigoletto); Callas (Gilda); di Stefano (Duke);
            Garcia (Maddalena); Ruffino (Sparafucile);
            Palacio de Bellas Artes Chorus and Orchestra;
            Mugnai (Conductor)

1954   Taddei (Rigoletto); Pagliughi (Gilda); Tagliavini (Duke); Colasanti (Maddalena);
            Neri (Sparafucile);
            Turin Radio Chorus and Orchestra;
            Questa (Conductor)

1954   Protti (Rigoletto); Gueden (Gilda); del Monaco (Duke); Simionato (Maddalena);
            Siepi (Sparafucile);
            Santa Cecilia Academy Chorus and Orchestra;
            Erede (Conductor)

1955   Gobbi (Rigoletto); Callas (Gilda); di Stefano (Duke); Lazzarini (Maddalena);
            Zaccaria (Sparafucile);
            La Scala Chorus and Orchestra;
            Serafin (Conductor)

1957   Merrill (Rigoletto); Peters (Gilda); Björling (Duke); Rota (Maddalena);
               Tozzi (Sparafucile);
               Rome Opera Chorus and Orchestra;
               Perlea (Conductor)

1959   Capecchi (Rigoletto); D'Angelo (Gilda); Tuckers (Duke); Pirazzini (Maddalena);
               Sardi (Sparafucile);
               San Carlo Opera Chorus and Orchestra;
               Molinari-Pradelli (Conductor)

1959   Hasslo (Rigoletto); Hallin (Gilda); Gedda (Duke); Meyer (Maddalena);
               Tyren (Sparafucile);
               Stockholm Royal Opera Chorus and Orchestra;
               Ehrling (Conductor)

1960   (In German)
               Ruzdiak (Rigoletto); Coertse (Gilda); Terkal (Duke); Wien (Maddalena);
               Hamburg Radio Chorus and Orchestra;
               Martin (Conductor)

1960   (In French)
               Massard (Rigoletto); Doria (Gilda); Vanzo (Duke); Scharley (Maddalena);
               Legros (Sparafucile);
               Etcheverry (Conductor)

1960   Bastianini (Rigoletto); Scotto (Gilda); Kraus (Duke); Cossotto (Maddalena);
               Vinco (Sparafucile);
               Florence Festival Chorus and Orchestra;
               Gavezzini (Conductor)

1961   MacNeil (Rigoletto); Sutherland (Gilda); Cioni (Duke); Malagù (Maddalena);
               Siepi (Sparafucile);
               Santa Cecilia Academy Chorus and Orchestra;
               Sanzogno (Conductor)

1962   Monachesi (Rigoletto); Benvenuti (Gilda); Rocchi (Duke); Pirazzini (Maddalena);
               Gambelli (Sparafucile);
               San Carlo Opera Chorus and Orchestra;
               Patané (Conductor)

1963   (In German)
               Gutstein (Rigoletto); Paller (Gilda); Curzi (Duke); Gust (Maddalena);
               Horn (Sparafucile);
               Bavarian State Opera Chorus and Orchestra;
               Galliera (Conductor)

1963   Concone (Rigoletto); Ratti (Gilda); Brevi (Duke); Freschi (Maddalena);
Botta (Sparafucile);
Patagonia Festival Chorus and Orchestra;
de Cross (Conductor)

1963   Fischer-Dieskau (Rigoletto); Scotto (Gilda); Bergonzi (Duke);
Cossotto (Maddalena); Testi (Sparafucile);
La Scala Chorus and Orchestra;
Kubelik (Conductor)

1963   Merrill (Rigoletto); Moffo (Gilda); Kraus (Duke); Elias (Maddalena);
Ward (Sparafucile);
RCA Italiana Chorus and Orchestra;
Solti (Conductor)

1963   Herlea (Rigoletto); Ianculescu (Gilda); Buzea (Duke); Palade (Maddalena);
Rafael (Sparafucile);
Bucharest National Opera Chorus and Orchestra;
Bobescu (Conductor)

1964   Montefusco (Rigoletto); Maccianti (Gilda); Molese (Duke);
Casei (Maddalena); Davia (Sparafucile);
Vienna State Opera Chorus and Orchestra;
Rivoli (Conductor)

1965   (In Hungarian)
Melis (Rigoletto); László (Gilda); Ilosfalvy (Duke);
Barlay (Maddalena); Bódy (Sparafucile);
Hungarian State Opera Chorus and Orchestra;
Gardelli (Conductor)

1967   MacNeil (Rigoletto); Grist (Gilda); Gedda (Duke); di Stasio (Maddalena);
Ferrin (Sparafucile);
Rome Opera Chorus and Orchestra;
Molinari-Pradelli (Conductor)

1972   Milnes (Rigoletto); Sutherland (Gilda); Pavarotti (Duke); Tourangeau (Maddalena);
Talvela (Sparafucile);
Ambrosian Opera Chorus/London Symphony Orchestra;
Bonynge (Conductor)

1977   Panerai (Rigoletto); Rinaldi (Gilda); Bonisolli (Duke); Cortez (Maddalena);
Rundgren (Sparafucile);
Dresden State Opera Chorus and Orchestra;
Molinari-Pradelli (Conductor)

1978   Milnes (Rigoletto); Sills (Gilda); Kraus (Duke); Dunn (Maddalena);
Ramey (Sparafucile);
Ambrosian Opera Chorus/Philharmonia Orchestra;
Rudel (Conductor)

1979   Cappuccilli (Rigoletto); Cortrubas (Gilda); Domingo (Duke);
Obraztsova (Maddalena); Ghiaurov (Sparafucile);
Vienna State Opera Chorus/Vienna Philharmonic Orchestra;
Giulini (Conductor)

1983   (In English)
Rawnsley (Rigoletto); Field (Gilda); Davies (Duke); Rigby (Maddalena);
Tomlinson (Sparafucile);
English National Opera Chorus and Orchestra;
Elder (Conductor)

1984   Bruson (Rigoletto); Gruberova (Gilda); Shicoff (Duke);
Fassbaender (Maddalena); Lloyd (Sparafucile);
Academy of Santa Cecilia Chorus and Orchestra;
Sinopoli (Conductor)

1988   Zancanaro (Rigoletto); Dessi (Gilda); la Scola (Duke); Senn (Maddalena);
Burchuladze (Sparafucile);
La Scala Chorus and Orchestra;
Muti (Conductor)

1989   Nucci (Rigoletto); Anderson (Gilda); Pavarotti (Duke); Verrett (Maddalena);
Ghiaurov (Sparafucile);
Bologna Teatro Communale Chorus and Orchestra;
Chailly (Conductor)

1994   Bruson (Rigoletto); Rost (Gilda); Alagna (Duke);
La Scala Chorus and Orchestra;
Muti (Conductor)

RIGOLETTO

Videography

DECCA VHS
>   Wixell (Rigoletto); Gruberova (Gilda); Pavarotti (Duke);
>   Vergara (Maddalena); Furlanetto (Sparafucile);
>   Vienna State Opera Chorus/Vienna Philharmonic Orchestra;
>   Chailly (Conductor);
>   A film by Jean-Pierre Ponnelle

THAMES VIDEO VHS
>   Rawnsley (Rigoletto); McLaughline (Gilda); Davies (Duke);
>   Rigby (Maddalena); Tomlinson (Sparafucile);
>   English National Opera Chorus and Orchestra;
>   Elder (Conductor);
>   Miller (Director);
>   Phillips (Video Director)

PICKWICK VHS
>   Gobbi (Rigoletto); Pagliughi (Gilda); Filippeschi (Duke);
>   Canala (Maddalena); Neri (Sparafucile);
>   Rome Opera Chorus and Orchestra;
>   Serafin (Conductor);
>   Gallone (Director)

DICTIONARY OF OPERA AND MUSICAL TERMS

Accelerando - Play the music faster, but gradually.

Adagio - At slow or gliding tempo, not as slow as Largo, but not as fast as Andante.

Agitato - Restless or agitated.

Allegro - At a brisk or lively tempo, faster than Andante but not as fast as Presto.

Andante - A moderately slow, easy-going tempo.

Appoggiatura - An extra or embellishing note preceding a main melodic note or tone. Usually written as a note of smaller size, it shares the time value of the main note.

Arabesque - Flourishes or fancy patterns usually applying to vocal virtuosity.

Aria - A solo song usually structured in a formal pattern. Arias generally convey reflective and introspective thoughts rather than descriptive action.

Arietta - A shortened form of aria.

Arioso - A musical passage or composition having a mixture of free recitative and metrical song.

Arpeggio - Producing the tones of a chord in succession but not simultaneously.

Atonal - Music that is not anchored in traditional musical tonality; it uses the chromatic scale impartially, does not use the diatonic scale and has no keynote or tonal center.

Ballad Opera - 18th century English opera consisting of spoken dialogue and music derived from popular ballad and folksong sources. The most famous is *The Beggar's Opera* which was a satire of the Italian opera seria.

Bar - A vertical line across the stave that divides the music into units.

Baritone - A male singing voice ranging between the bass and tenor.

Baroque - A style of artistic expression prevalent in the 17th century that is marked generally by the use of complex forms, bold ornamentation, and florid decoration. The Baroque period extends from approximately 1600 to 1750 and includes the works of the original creators of modern opera, the Camerata, as well as the later works by Bach and Handel.

Bass - The lowest male voices, usually divided into categories such as:

> **Basso buffo** - A bass voice that specializes in comic roles like Dr. Bartolo in Rossini's *The Barber of Seville.*

> **Basso cantante** - A bass voice that demonstrates melodic singing quality rather than comic or tragic: King Philip in Verdi's *Don Carlos.*

> **Basso profundo** - the deepest, most profound, or most dramatic of bass voices: Sarastro in Mozart's *The Magic Flute.*

Bel canto - Literally "beautiful singing." It originated in Italian opera of the 17th and 18th centuries and stressed beautiful tones produced with ease, clarity, purity, evenness, together with an agile vocal technique and virtuosity. Bel canto flourished in the first half of the 19th century in the works of Rossini, Bellini, and Donizetti.

Cabaletta - Typically a lively bravura extension of an aria or duet that creates a climax. The term is derived from the Italian word "cavallo," or horse: it metaphorically describes a horse galloping to the finish line.

Cadenza - A flourish or brilliant part of an aria commonly inserted just before a finale.

Camerata - A gathering of Florentine writers and musicians between 1590 and 1600 who attempted to recreate what they believed was the ancient Greek theatrical synthesis of drama, music, and stage spectacle; their experimentation led to the creation of the early structural forms of modern opera.

Cantabile - An expression indication urging the singer to sing sweetly.

Cantata - A choral piece generally containing Scriptural narrative texts: Bach Cantatas.

Cantilena - A lyrical melodic line meant to be played or sung "cantabile," or with sweetness and expression.

Canzone - A short, lyrical operatic song usually containing no narrative association with the drama but rather simply reflecting the character's state of mind: Cherubino's "Voi che sapete" in Mozart's *The Marriage of Figaro.* Shorter versions are called canzonettas.

Castrato - A young male singer who was surgically castrated to retain his treble voice.

Cavatina - A short aria popular in the 18th century without the da capo repeat section.

Classical Period - The period between the Baroque and Romantic periods. The Classical period is generally considered to have begun with the birth of Mozart (1756) and ended with Beethoven's death (1830). Stylistically, the music of the period stressed clarity, precision, and rigid structural forms.

Coda - A trailer or tailpiece added on by the composer after the music's natural conclusion.

Coloratura - Literally colored: it refers to a soprano singing in the bel canto tradition with great agility, virtuosity, embellishments and ornamentation: Joan Sutherland singing in Donizetti's *Lucia di Lammermoor.*

Commedia dell'arte - A popular form of dramatic presentation originating in Renaissance Italy in which highly stylized characters were involved in comic plots involving mistaken identities and misunderstandings. The standard characters were Harlequin and Colombine: The "play within a play" in Leoncavallo's *I Pagliacci.*

Comprimario - A singer portraying secondary character roles such as confidantes, servants, and messengers.

Continuo - A bass part (as for a keyboard or stringed instrument) that was used especially in baroque ensemble music; it consists of a succession of bass notes with figures that indicate the required chords. Also called *figured bass, thoroughbass.*

Contralto - The lowest female voice derived from "contra" against, and "alto" voice, a voice between the tenor and mezzo-soprano.

Countertenor, or male alto vocal range - A high male voice generally singing within the female high soprano ranges.

Counterpoint - The combination of one or more independent melodies added into a single harmonic texture in which each retains its linear character: polyphony. The most sophisticated form of counterpoint is the fugue form in which up to 6 to 8 voices are combined, each providing a variation on the basic theme but each retaining its relation to the whole.

Crescendo - A gradual increase in the volume of a musical passage.

Da capo - Literally "from the top": repeat. Early 17th century da capo arias were in the form of A B A, the last A section repeating the first A section.

Deus ex machina - Literally "god out of a machine." A dramatic technique in which a person or thing appears or is introduced suddenly and unexpectedly; it provides a contrived solution to an apparently insoluble dramatic difficulty.

Diatonic - Relating to a major or minor musical scale that comprises intervals of five whole steps and two half steps.

Diminuendo - Gradually getting softer, the opposite of crescendo.

Dissonance - A mingling of discordant sounds that do not harmonize within the diatonic scale.

Diva - Literally a "goddess"; generally refers to a female opera star who either possesses, or pretends to possess, great rank.

Dominant - The fifth tone of the diatonic scale: in the key of C, the dominant is G.

Dramma giocoso - Literally meaning amusing, or lighthearted. Like tragicomedy it represents an opera whose story combines both serious and comic elements: Mozart's *Don Giovanni.*

Falsetto - Literally a lighter or "false" voice; an artificially produced high singing voice that extends above the range of the full voice.

Fioritura - Literally "flower"; a flowering ornamentation or embellishment of the vocal line within an aria.

Forte, Fortissimo - Forte (*f*) means loud: mezzo forte (*mf*) is fairly loud; fortissimo (*ff*) even louder, and additional *fff*'s indicate greater degrees of loudness.

Glissando - A rapid sliding up or down the scale.

Grand Opera - An opera in which there is no spoken dialogue and the entire text is set to music, frequently treating serious and dramatic subjects. Grand Opera flourished in France in the 19th century (Meyerbeer) and most notably by Verdi (Aida): the genre is epic in scale and combines spectacle, large choruses, scenery, and huge orchestras.

Heldentenor - A tenor with a powerful dramatic voice who possesses brilliant top notes and vocal stamina. Heldentenors are well suited to heroic (Wagnerian) roles: Lauritz Melchoir in Wagner's *Tristan und Isolde.*

Imbroglio - Literally "Intrigue"; an operatic scene with chaos and confusion and appropriate diverse melodies and rhythms.

Largo or larghetto - Largo indicates a very slow tempo; Larghetto is slightly faster than Largo.

Legato - Literally "tied"; therefore, successive tones that are connected smoothly. Opposing Legato would be Marcato (strongly accented and punctuated) and Staccato (short and aggressive).

Leitmotif - A short musical passage attached to a person, thing, feeling, or idea that provides associations when it recurs or is recalled.

Libretto - Literally "little book"; the text of an opera. On Broadway, the text of songs is called "lyrics" but the spoken text in the play is called the "book."

Lied - A German song; the plural is "lieder." Originally German art songs of the 19th century.

Light opera, or operetta - Operas that contain comic elements but light romantic plots: Johann Strauss's *Die Fledermaus.*

Maestro - From the Italian "master": a term of respect to conductors, composers, directors, and great musicians.

Melodrama - Words spoken over music. Melodrama appears in Beethoven's *Fidelio* but flourished during the late 19th century in the operas of Massenet (*Manon*). Melodrama should not be confused with melodrama when it describes a work that is characterized by extravagant theatricality and by the predominance of plot and physical action over characterization.

Mezza voce - Literally "medium voice," or singing with medium or half volume; it is generally intended as a vocal means to intensify emotion.

Mezzo-soprano - A woman's voice with a range between that of the soprano and contralto.

Molto - Very. Molto agitato means very agitated.

Obbligato - An elaborate accompaniment to a solo or principal melody that is usually played by a single instrument.

Octave - A musical interval embracing eight diatonic degrees: therefore, from C to C is an octave.

Opera - Literally "a work"; a dramatic or comic play combining music.

Opera buffa - Italian comic opera that flourished during the bel canto era. Buffo characters were usually basses singing patter songs: Dr. Bartolo in Rossini's *The Barber of Seville,* and Dr. Dulcamara in Donizetti's *The Elixir of Love.*

Opéra comique - A French opera characterized by spoken dialogue interspersed between the arias and ensemble numbers, as opposed to Grand Opera in which there is no spoken dialogue.

Operetta, or light opera - Operas that contain comic elements but tend to be more romantic: Strauss's *Die Fledermaus,* Offenbach's *La Périchole,* and Lehar's *The Merry Widow.* In operettas, there is usually much spoken dialogue, dancing, practical jokes, and mistaken identities.

Oratorio - A lengthy choral work, usually of a religious or philosophical nature and consisting chiefly of recitatives, arias, and choruses but in deference to its content, performed without action or scenery: Handel's *Messiah.*

Ornamentation - Extra embellishing notes—appoggiaturas, trills, roulades, or cadenzas—that enhance a melodic line.

Overture - The orchestral introduction to a musical dramatic work that frequently incorporates musical themes within the work.

Parlando - Literally "speaking"; the imitation of speech while singing, or singing that is almost speaking over the music. It is usually short and with minimal orchestral accompaniment.

Patter - Words rapidly and quickly delivered. Figaro's Largo in Rossini's *The Barber of Seville* is a patter song.

Pentatonic - A five-note scale, like the black notes within an octave on the piano.

Piano - Soft volume.

Pitch - The property of a musical tone that is determined by the frequency of the waves producing it.

Pizzicato - A passage played by plucking the strings instead of stroking the string with the bow.

Polyphony - Literally "many voices." A style of musical composition in which two or more independent melodies are juxtaposed in harmony; counterpoint.

Polytonal - The use of several tonal schemes simultaneously.

Portamento - A continuous gliding movement from one tone to another.

Prelude - An orchestral introduction to an act or the whole opera. An Overture can appear only at the beginning of an opera.

Presto, Prestissimo - Very fast and vigorous.

Prima Donna - The female star of an opera cast. Although the term was initially used to differentiate between the dramatic and vocal importance of a singer, today it generally describes the personality of a singer rather than her importance in the particular opera.

Prologue - A piece sung before the curtain goes up on the opera proper: Tonio's Prologue in Leoncavallo's *I Pagliacci*.

Quaver - An eighth note.

Range - The divisions of the voice: soprano, mezzo-soprano, contralto, tenor, baritone, and bass.

Recitative - A formal device that that advances the plot. It is usually a rhythmically free vocal style that imitates the natural inflections of speech; it represents the dialogue and narrative in operas and oratorios. Secco recitative is accompanied by harpsichord and sometimes with cello or continuo instruments and *accompagnato* indicates that the recitative is accompanied by the orchestra.

Ritornello - A short recurrent instrumental passage between elements of a vocal composition.

Romanza - A solo song that is usually sentimental; it is usually shorter and less complex than an aria and rarely deals with terror, rage, and anger.

Romantic Period - The period generally beginning with the raiding of the Bastille (1789) and the last revolutions and uprisings in Europe (1848). Romanticists generally found inspiration in nature and man. Beethoven's *Fidelio* (1805) is considered the first Romantic opera, followed by the works of Verdi and Wagner.

Roulade - A florid vocal embellishment sung to one syllable.

Rubato - Literally "robbed"; it is a fluctuation of tempo within a musical phrase, often against a rhythmically steady accompaniment.

Secco - The accompaniment for recitative played by the harpsichord and sometimes continuo instruments.

Semitone - A half-step, the smallest distance between two notes. In the key of C, the notes are E and F, and B and C.

Serial music - Music based on a series of tones in a chosen pattern without regard for traditional tonality.

Sforzando - Sudden loudness and force; it must stick out from the texture and provide a shock.

Singspiel - Early German musical drama employing spoken dialogue between songs: Mozart's *The Magic Flute.*

Soprano - The highest range of the female voice ranging from lyric (light and graceful quality) to dramatic (fuller and heavier in tone).

Sotto voce - Literally "below the voice"; sung softly between a whisper and a quiet conversational tone.

Soubrette - A soprano who sings supporting roles in comic opera: Adele in Strauss's *Die Fledermaus*, or Despina in Mozart's *Così fan tutte.*

Spinto - From the Italian "spingere" (to push); a soprano having lyric vocal qualities who "pushes" the voice to achieve heavier dramatic qualities.

Sprechstimme - Literally "speak voice." The singer half sings a note and half speaks; the declamation sounds like speaking but the duration of pitch makes it seem almost like singing.

Staccato - Short, clipped, rapid articulation; the opposite of the caressing effects of legato.

Stretto - A concluding passage performed in a quicker tempo to create a musical climax.

Strophe - Music repeated for each verse of an aria.

Syncopation - Shifting the beat forward or back from its usual place in the bar; it is a temporary displacement of the regular metrical accent in music caused typically by stressing the weak beat.

Supernumerary - A "super"; a performer with a non-singing role: "Spear-carrier."

Tempo - Time, or speed. The ranges are Largo for very slow to Presto for very fast.

Tenor - Highest natural male voice.

Tessitura - The general range of a melody or voice part; but specifically, the part of the register in which most of the tones of a melody or voice part lie.

Tonality - The organization of all the tones and harmonies of a piece of music in relation to a tonic (the first tone of its scale).

Tone Poem - An orchestral piece with a program; a script.

Tonic - The keynote of the key in which a piece is written. C is the tonic of C major.

Trill - Two adjacent notes rapidly and repeatedly alternated.

Tutti - All together.

Twelve tone - The 12 chromatic tones of the octave placed in a chosen fixed order and constituting with some permitted permutations and derivations the melodic and harmonic material of a serial musical piece. Each note of the chromatic scale is used as part of the melody before any other note gets repeated.

Verismo - Literally "truth"; the artistic use of contemporary everyday material in preference to the heroic or legendary in opera. A movement from the late 19th century: *Carmen.*

Vibrato - A "vibration"; a slightly tremulous effect imparted to vocal or instrumental tone for added warmth and expressiveness by slight and rapid variations in pitch.